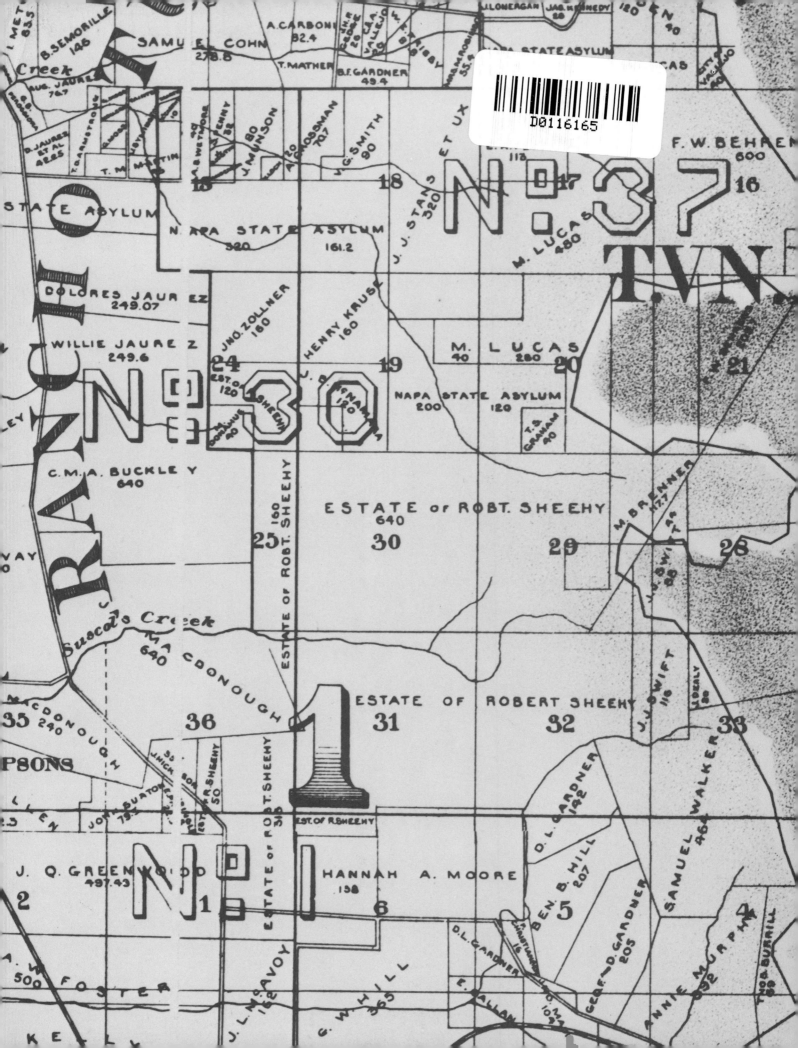

By
Denzil Verardo, Ph.D.
and Jennie Dennis Verardo

"Partners in Progress" by
Nancy J. Hutchins

Produced in Cooperation with the
Napa County Historical Society

Windsor Publications, Inc.
Northridge, California

*Napa Valley artist E. John Robinson captures the majestic
beauty of the valley in his oil painting titled* Harvest Gold.
*Courtesy, Barbara W. Ryan, The Gallery on Main Street, St.
Helena, California*

Napa Valley

From golden fields to purple harvest

Windsor Publications, Inc.—History Book Division
Publisher: John M. Phillips
Staff for *Napa Valley: From Golden Fields to Purple Harvest*
Editorial Director: Teri Davis Greenberg
Editorial Assistants: Laura Cordova, Marilyn Horn, Marcie Goldstein
Design Director: Alexander D'Anca
Designer: Christina McKibbin
Layout Artist: J.R. Vasquez
Director, Corporate Biographies: Karen Story
Assistant Director, Corporate Biographies: Phyllis Gray
Editorial Assistants, Corporate Biographies: Kathy M. Brown, Pat Pittman, Sharon Volz
Sales Representatives, Corporate Biographies: Jacquie Carroll and Larry Yurdin

Library of Congress Cataloging in Publication Data

Verardo, Denzil.
   Napa Valley: from golden fields to purple harvest.

   Bibliography: p. 157
   Includes index.
   1. Napa River Valley (Calif.)—History. 2. Napa
River Valley (Calif.)—Description and travel. 3. Napa
River Valley (Calif.)—Industries. I. Verardo, Jennie
Dennis. II. Napa County Historical Society. III. Title.
F868.N2V47   1986   979.4'19   86-9108
ISBN 0-89781-164-X

Endsheets: *Former Napa County Surveyor O.H. Buckman's official records and surveys were used to draw an Official Map of the County of Napa, California, which was published in 1895. Reproduced here are two details from the two-part map, in which each part measures about 34 x 46 inches. Courtesy, Library of Congress, Geography and Map Division*

CONTENTS

PREFACE

7

NAPA VALLEY THROUGH TIME: A CHRONOLOGY

8

CHAPTER ONE

LIFE BEFORE THE PLOW

11

CHAPTER TWO

CONFLICT AND CHANGE

27

CHAPTER THREE

THE CRUSH IS ON

45

CHAPTER FOUR

SPIRIT, MIND, AND VOICE

61

CHAPTER FIVE

ROCKCRUSHERS, RESORTS, "HEATHENS," AND A "HERETIC"

79

CHAPTER SIX

CHANGING VISTAS

93

CHAPTER SEVEN

PARTNERS IN PROGRESS

113

PATRONS

156

BIBLIOGRAPHY

157

INDEX

158

To Mark
For your patience and perseverance, and for skillfully performing
the difficult task of being our son

Local artist Don Hatfield depicts a nostalgic valley scene in his idyllic oil painting titled In the Mustard. *Courtesy, Barbara W. Ryan, The Gallery on Main Street, St. Helena, California*

PREFACE

Anyone who has lived in the Napa Valley gains an appreciation of its history. Even the casual visitor cannot help but be lured into the valley's past, whether by viewing the spectacular architecture of its wineries and color of its vineyards, or the awesome waterwheel at Bale's Grist Mill, or by experiencing the quiet solitude of Robert Louis Stevenson Memorial State Park.

We have written this work with the goal of enhancing that experience by providing a detailed, but flowing account of the Napa Valley's past. In *Napa Valley: From Golden Fields to Purple Harvest,* we did not pretend to write a definitive history, but we hope we have written an accurate, enjoyable one, presenting up-to-date research material and carefully selected photographs.

Much of the history of the Napa Valley is reflective of what was occurring throughout California. However, many of the historical events that occurred in the Napa Valley determined the destiny of the state itself. Thus the valley's history is much more than a small, mirror-image of California history. It is more than a reflection. Indeed, to read and study the history of the Napa Valley is to gain an understanding of those events around which much of California's history revolved. An aim of this work is to highlight those events and individuals in the Napa Valley that played an important part in that California experience.

While, as residents of the Napa Valley, we fell in love with its beauty, as historians, we appreciate its past. As authors, we hope to leave the reader with an understanding of those forces that shaped its destiny.

As always with an undertaking of this magnitude, there are those without whom the task would have been much more difficult. We first and foremost express our appreciation and respect for Jess Doud. He has served the Napa County Historical Society, both as president and executive director, longer than any other individual. His assistance and knowledge have been invaluable. His courtesy in allowing us archival access at times convenient to our schedule, and not necessarily his, made our research task as simple and complete as one could hope for.

The board of directors of the Napa County Historical Society made this work possible through their sponsorship and open support of our project.

Without Brother Timothy of the Christian Brothers, we could not have secured the cover illustration for our book. For locating, shipping, and copying the painting used for the cover within our deadline schedule, we owe Brother Timothy our thanks. He is a joy to work with.

Another individual whose assistance was invaluable was Steven Klein, assistant library director of the Napa City-County Library. We were not only allowed access to virtually all materials available in the library's collections, but also received gracious assistance from the library staff.

The following individuals and institutions also assisted us, directly or indirectly, with *Napa Valley: From Golden Fields to Purple Harvest:* The California Department of Parks and Recreation, John Wichels, Jack and Elayne Hesemeyer, Bill Krumbein, Richard McKillop, the California State Library, Grace Baker of the Society of California Pioneers, Norman Wilson, Paula Peterson, the California Historical Society, and Teri Davis Greenberg, our editor.

Last, but by no means least, we thank Mark Verardo, our research assistant.

Denzil and Jennie Verardo

NAPA VALLEY THROUGH TIME
A CHRONOLOGY

2000 B.C.-1823 The Wappo Indians were the sole inhabitants of the Napa Valley.

1823 Don Francisco Castro and Father José Altimura, under an armed escort led by José Sanchez, became the first Europeans to explore the Napa Valley.

182? Guy Fling was the first American to explore the Napa Valley sometime during the 1820s.

1829 Kit Carson entered the Napa Valley while on a hunting trip.

1831 Guy Fling led Napa County's first settler, George C. Yount, into the Napa Valley.

1836 First treaty in California between the natives and the Mexicans was drawn up.
George C. Yount was awarded the first land grant in the Napa Valley, Rancho Caymus.
George Yount built the area's first permanent dwelling, a wooden blockhouse.

1837 Dr. Edward Turner Bale came to California from England.

1838 A smallpox epidemic raged through Napa County killing hundreds of Wappo Indians.

1840 Cayetano Juarez built two adobes on his Rancho Tulucay and moved his family from Sonoma into them.

1841 Dr. Edward Turner Bale became a citizen of Mexico and was granted Rancho Carne Humana, which comprised the land between present-day Rutherford and Calistoga.

1844 Colonel Joseph B. Chiles, who guided one of the earliest immigrant trains to California, was granted Rancho Catacula in the Napa Valley.
The first landing of a ship in what would become Napa City occurred. The ship was called the *Sacramento*.

1845 James Clyman, mountain man, journeyed to the Napa Valley.

1846 The Bale Grist Mill was completed.
The Donner Party became trapped in a Sierra snowfall; Napa settlers aided in rescuing the survivors.
Ezekial Merritt left John C. Frémont's camp in Sacramento bound for Sonoma to revolt against Mexican rule. The Bear Flag party was formed.
The Bear Flag Rebellion took place in Sonoma; the California Republic was formed with the "bear flag" as its symbol.

1848 The Town of Napa was founded by Nathan Coombs.
Napa's first structure, a saloon, was built by Harrison Pierce.
James Marshall discovered gold in California; Napa City was deserted as residents flocked to the mines.

1849 Napa County formed as one of California's original counties.
Edward Turner Bale died.
The first school opened in the Napa Valley with the class taught by Sarah Graves Fosdick, a survivor of the Donner Party.

1850 The *Dolphin* became the first steamship to navigate the Napa River.
Napa County's first officers were elected.

1852 Napa County's board of supervisors created the townships of Napa, Yount, and Hot Springs.

1853 The community of St. Helena was established.
The Napa Valley's first church building was erected. It was Methodist in denomination.

1856 The Napa County *Reporter* opened its doors as the county's first newspaper.

1858 A silver rush occurred in Napa County, and the mining era began.
Napa County's first Catholic Church was erected in Napa City.
Charles Krug produced 1,200 gallons of wine in the Napa Valley using a small cider press.

1859 Sam Brannan purchased land in the upper Napa Valley; the purchase included the land on which Calistoga would be developed.

1860 Charles Krug married Dr. Bale's daughter, Caroline.
Charles Krug planted grapes on land north of St. Helena, land which had been Caroline Bale's dowry.
The Napa Collegiate Institute opened. It was a forerunner of today's University of the Pacific in Stockton.
Cinnabar, mercury ore, was discovered in Napa County.

1861 The Phoenix Mining Company was organized to extract mercury from cinnabar.
A severe winter hit the Napa Valley exterminating most of the area's cattle herds.

1863-1865 A drought struck the Napa Valley.

1863 The Napa *Register* was founded.

1864 The Napa Valley Railroad began operation.
Napa County became one of California's leading quicksilver (mercury) producers.

1865 George Yount, Napa County's first anglo settler, died.

1866 John Lawley began his toll road.

1867 The telegraph line to Napa was extended from Napa

to Calistoga.

The Napa City Gas Light Company was incorporated to provide lighting on the streets of Napa; Napa became the tenth city in California to be lit by gas.

1868 Central School in Napa became the county's first eight-year grammar school.

1869 The Sawyer Tanning Company was established.

1870 The first library in Napa was opened by the Napa Library Association.

1872 The Town of Napa City was incorporated.

1873 The Seventh Day Adventist Church was organized in Napa.

1874 The Town of Napa City was reincorporated as the City of Napa.

The First Presbyterian Church in Napa was erected.

The *St. Helena Star* was founded.

Eadweard Muybridge, the "Father of the Motion Picture," was tried for murder and acquitted in the City of Napa.

1875 The St. Helena Viticultural Club organized with Charles Krug as its first president.

1876 The Napa State Asylum for the Insane received its first patients.

1877 The *Calistogan* was founded. Jacob and Frederick Beringer established the Beringer Bros. Winery.

1878 The St. Helena Sanitarium was founded.

1879 The Bale Grist Mill ground grain for the last time with its thirty-six-foot waterwheel.

1880 Robert Louis Stevenson arrived in the Napa Valley.

1881 James Clyman died and was buried in Napa's Tulocay Cemetery.

1883 Robert Louis Stevenson's *Silverado Squatters* was published.

Robert Louis Stevensons's *Treasure Island* was published.

The Napa City Water Company was founded by Samuel Holden.

Cayetano Juarez died and was buried in the Tulocay Cemetery on land which he had donated to the City of Napa.

The first telephone service reached Napa.

Napa County imposed fixed salaries for its justices of the peace.

1884 The California Veteran's Home in Yountville was opened.

1887 Electric service was installed in the City of Napa.

1888 The Palisades Mine began operation.

1891 Charles Krug died.

1893 Half of the vineyards in the Napa Valley had become infested with the plant louse, phylloxera.

Napa County's first high school opened in St. Helena.

1894 The St. Helena Library opened.

1897 The State of California assumed administration of the California Veteran's Home.

1902 The Calistoga Free Public Library opened.

The Napa Valley Railroad Company, an electric railroad, was incorporated and ran from Benecia to Calistoga.

1903 The Napa Glove Factory was organized. It was the largest glove factory west of Chicago.

1909 500,000 fruit and nut trees had been established in the valley by this date.

1910 Napa City's first hospital, the Shurtleff Hospital, opened.

1915 The loudspeaker was invented in Napa by Edwin Pridham and Peter Jensen.

1916 The County Library System was established.

1917 Bruce Land of Napa became the first Napa Countian drafted in World War I.

1920 Prohibition went into effect; many Napa Valley wineries went out of business.

1922 The Lawley toll road was purchased by the county. It became State Highway 29.

1923 Millikan Dam was begun.

1924 The Napa State Asylum for the Insane was renamed Napa State Hospital.

Giuseppe Musante first bottled water. His company would be the forerunner of the Calistoga Mineral Water Company.

1929 The steam train made its last run up the Napa Valley.

1932 The Christian Brothers moved their novitiate and wine-making operation to the Napa Valley.

1933 Prohibition was repealed.

1939 By this date the Sawyer Tanning Company of Napa was the largest tannery west of the Mississippi.

1948 Conn Dam was completed.

1953 5,500,000 gallons of wine were produced in the Napa Valley.

1950s Controversial plans to flood the Berryessa Valley as part of the California Water Project were completed.

1963 Over 500,000 people visited the Napa Valley's wineries.

1968 The Calistoga Soaring Center opened.

The County Board of Supervisors created agricultural preserve zoning restrictions.

1976-1977 A severe drought struck the Napa Valley; water rationing took place in several of the county's communities.

1981 The Calistoga Mineral Water Company was purchased by the French firm, Perrier.

1983 Over 400,000 people toured the Christian Brothers Greystone Winery.

1985 The seventieth anniversary of the invention of the loudspeaker in Napa was celebrated.

The *Napa Valley Times* issued its inaugural edition on July 25. The premiere edition of the *Napa Sentinal* was published on September 20.

The Wine Train began its run in December.

1986 In mid-February continuous rain flooded valley communities and inundated vineyards, about a decade after the area experienced a severe drought.

The geothermal activity in the Calistoga area of the valley seems as prevalent today as it was centuries ago.

Chapter 1

LIFE BEFORE THE PLOW

The Napa Valley has a long and colorful history of explanations of its name. One source credits the area's Indians with un-equalled bravery and points to the Pomo Indian word "napa" meaning "harpoon point" as having some connection with their martial skills. Others cite the definition of "near home" or "motherland" and the Indian tradition that the Napa Valley was the cradle of the Suisun race. An early historian, C. A. Menefee, said that the word "napa" meant "fish" and that "it was given to this section on account of the great numbers of finny tribes that infested the streams and brooks and afforded the dwellers inland a bountiful supply of food." Still another explanation maintains that "napa" means

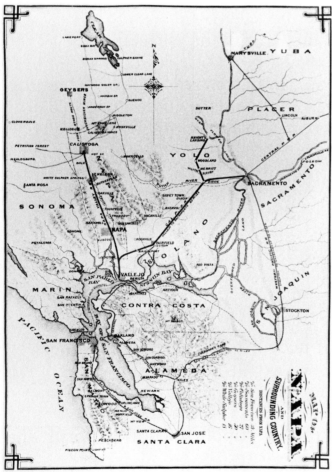

Above: *The Napa Valley has been a destination for travellers since before the turn of the century. This 1878 map shows its location in Northern California and includes major transportation routes. Courtesy, Napa County Historical Society*

Top: *Mount St. Helena is pictured here from a point on Highway 128. Father José Altimura may have named the mountain after Saint Helena; Russians from Fort Ross may have named it for their country's patron saint; or an American sea captain may have christened it after the ship* St. Helena.

"grizzly bear" and while there seemed to have been an abundance of these creatures in the valley, this definition is one of the least-often mentioned. Spellings have ranged from "Nappa" and "napa" to the current "Napa." Fortunately the valley's story is more easily explained than its name.

Napa County is one of the original twenty-seven counties formed in California in 1850. It is characterized by the Napa River Valley, as well as the valley's surrounding mountain ranges and smaller adjoining intermountain valleys. The history of Napa County is predominantly that of the Napa Valley, and for historical purposes the two can be considered synonymous.

The Napa Valley's destiny was molded during prehistoric times. Until recent years, Mount St. Helena was thought to be an extinct volcano. While that supposition has not proved to be true, there is no doubt that much of the valley was of volcanic origin. Geothermal activity in the Calistoga area seems to be as prevalent today as it was when early man first entered the valley. The naturally heated mineral waters still form a basis for the resort industry of the upper Napa Valley. Pumice, obsidian, and ancient lava terraces are obvious formations throughout Napa County and also serve as reminders of prehistoric volcanic action. Glass Mountain, on the eastern side of the valley between Calistoga and St. Helena, was formed by a flow of molten glass which poured out of the earth's interior during the era of volcanoes. Of the minerals found in the county, many were deposited during this period. Gold, silver, and cinnabar were all present in the area in sufficient abundance to cause the rise, and eventual fall, of industries devoted to their procurement. This geologic wealth served to attract habitation.

Through the geologic processes of sedimentation, folding, faulting, uplifting, and erosion, the base of today's rich soils was formed. It is the fertility of these soils that has made the Napa Valley famous agriculturally. The original wild oats that gave way to harvested wheat, the turn-of-the-century prune orchards, and the modern wine industry all owe some of their success to the valley's rich earth.

The Napa Valley is situated geographically with the San Pablo portion of San Francisco Bay as one boundary and the 4,334-foot Mount St. Helena as the other. The forty-mile long Napa River, which cuts through the valley, often reaches flood stage during the winter months. It is a major physical feature of the county, flowing from the head of the valley to the sloughs and tidal marshes of San Pablo Bay. The river is navigable as far up as the city of Napa, a fact important in the county's commercial history.

Warm summers and mild winters characterize the climate of the county. Summer heat, which in the upper Napa Valley near Calistoga can reach the 100 degree range, is moderated in the late evening and early morning by cooling air and fog common in the lower valley. This Mediterranean climate, rich soil, and availability of water induced settlement.

The climatically agreeable and naturally abundant valley has been inhabited for approximately 4,000 years and perhaps longer. Early

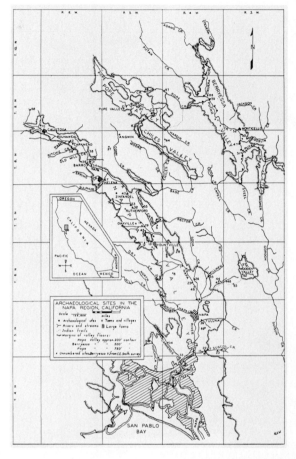

A 1947 archaeological expedition of the Napa region covered 1,188 square miles and yielded information on the early inhabitants of the area—the Patwin and Wappo tribes. The southern and eastern limits of the study were occupied by the Patwin, whose main territory was the western Sacramento Valley. Wappo country comprised the remainder of the area studied. This map shows archaeological sites and Patwin and Wappo towns and villages. From The Archaeology of the Napa Region, University of California Press: Berkeley, 1953

residents were predominantly members of the Wappo tribe. Their name, from an Americanization of the Spanish "guapo" meaning "brave," was earned during the mission period because of their stubborn resistance to domination and sublimation by the Franciscan padres at Mission Sonoma. A nomadic people, the Wappo lived simple lives and migrated as often and as far as necessary to find adequate food and shelter. There appear to have been six tribelets living in the area, each with its own dialect

Established in 1812 by the Russian American Company, Fort Ross posed a major threat to Spanish and Mexican California. It represented the continuing expansion of the Russian empire southward into California at a time when Spanish and Mexican authorities were attempting to maintain their dominance in the area. Reproduced at top is Old Fort Ross As Seen From the Hill, Res. of G.W. Call, Sonoma County, California *and at bottom is the chapel at Fort Ross after restoration from damage in the 1906 earthquake. Courtesy, The Bancroft Library, University of California, Berkeley and the Pat Hathaway Collection*

and at least one permanent village, but all sharing the Napa Valley and surrounding territory (present-day Lake, Sonoma, and Solano counties) with relatively few conflicts.

Early European descriptions of these natives labelled them "digger" Indians and most treated them with contempt or disgust. They were portrayed as uncivilized savages digging in the dirt for food and having few, if any, redeeming characteristics. It is now evident that while the Wappo did not have a technically developed life-style as did some Plains and eastern American Indians, they were not lacking the intelligence for development. Rather, they lacked the need. Food was plentiful so they were not required to develop agricultural skills. Beasts of burden were absent because it was not necessary to traverse great distances to secure food or shelter. Prior to European exploration, martial skills appear to have been somewhat limited due to an absence of intensive warfare.

The Wappo did not have a written language however, and in their sweathouses, stories, tradi-

In 1823 Mission San Francisco de Solano was established in Sonoma to aid in the protection and settlement of Spain's northern frontier, which included the Napa Valley. Later neglected, the mission fell into disrepair as it appears in this circa 1880 photo. Since restored, the mission is part of Sonoma State Historic Park. Courtesy, Pat Hathaway Collection

tions, and expectations were verbally passed on to the new generations of Wappo men. Though they had no churches or shrines, like many Indian peoples the Wappo's way of life was their religion. They attempted to live in harmony with the universe, and prayers and rituals were continually employed to achieve this goal. Into this idyllic setting marched the Spanish.

The land which today comprises Napa County was on the fringe of Spain's global empire. It was explored and opened to settlement in large part due to the international political situation at the beginning of the eighteenth century. In 1493, to keep peace between Spain and Portugal, the two leading world powers of that day, Pope Alexander VI had issued the Papal decision which divided the world between them. It is significant for Napa County history that Spain was given the Western Hemisphere. Spain then began an era of exploration which resulted in its court becoming the richest in Europe. Spanish galleons laden with treasure sailed the waters from the Philippines to Mexico by way

of California's coast. By the late 1700s, however, the security of California, which was of paramount importance to Spain, seemed in jeopardy.

England had been victorious in Canada and her sailors freely pirated the slow-moving galleons. Foreign trappers were venturing down from Canada into California itself. Russia was expanding southward from Alaska in its search for valuable sea otter pelts. Fort Ross, about 100 miles north of the Golden Gate, was established as a Russian outpost in 1812, and was of no small concern to the Spanish. At one point Spain's empire had seemed to be waning, but in 1759 Charles III became king

Above: *The Tulocay Cemetery in Napa is the final resting place for many of the West's earliest pioneers. Included are such notable Californians as the Grigsby family, mountain man James Clyman, and Californio Cayetano Juarez, who held one of the Napa Valley's earliest land grants. Courtesy, Denzil and Jennie Verardo*

Facing page: *Cayetano Juarez, shown here with his grandson Roy, served in the Mexican army in the 1830s. In 1841 he received the Rancho Tulucay grant, upon which a part of the city of Napa grew. Juarez was one of the first settlers in the valley, moving his family into a small adobe house on his grant. Courtesy, Napa County Historical Society*

George C. Yount. Yount, born in North Carolina in 1794, had fought with Andrew Jackson at the Battle of New Orleans and in the Seminole War. Taken prisoner by the Indians, he had actually been bound to the stake but managed to get free. Following his escape, he had been a hunter and trapper and an Indian fighter at large in the new frontier of the West.

Yount came to California from New Mexico with the William Wolfskill expedition in 1831. During that year he hunted otter and trapped beaver, proceeding to the missions of San Rafael and Sonoma toward the end of the year. It was purportedly while on one of Yount's otter expeditions that Guy Fling, the first American to explore the Napa Valley, piloted Yount into the valley. George Yount's handiwork and carpentry skills were invaluable to the padres at the missions, and he was soon employed by General Vallejo to make shingles for Vallejo's new house in Sonoma. Yount remained in Sonoma until 1835, aiding General Vallejo and teaching the local Indians the use of European tools. In 1835 Yount was baptized into the Catholic Church at Mission San Rafael under the name of Jorgé Concepcion Yount, presumably since Mexican citizenship and acceptance into the Catholic faith were two of the requirements necessary to receive land grants in California during this period. Yount travelled to the Napa Valley in 1835 and, through the influence of General Mariano Vallejo, was given the grant of Rancho Caymus on February 23, 1836. This grant consisted of two square leagues (11,814 acres) of land, which included the heart of the Napa Valley from the northern edge of present-day Yountville to the center of the valley.

George Yount was also the first settler to build a permanent dwelling between Sonoma and the settlements on the Columbia River.

His wooden blockhouse served as both a dwelling and a fort. It consisted of an upper room he used as living quarters and a lower one with portholes, through which he could defend himself from Indian raids. In 1837 Yount replaced his wooden cabin with an adobe fort and soon after erected a flour mill and a sawmill. He also stocked his rancho with several hundred head of cattle. A second grant, known as Rancho de la Jota, was made to Yount on October 21, 1843, and comprised almost a square league of timber on Howell Mountain, north of his Rancho Caymus. Yount probably used the timber from Rancho de la Jota to feed his sawmill. The community of Angwin, Pacific Union College, and the St. Helena Hospital and Health Center stand upon this former land grant.

Yount's Rancho Caymus became a regular stopping place for later immigrant parties whom he greeted with great hospitality. George Yount lived on his rancho until his death in 1865. It is difficult to assess Yount's influence on the later settlement of the Napa Valley, but his presence was of great importance to Alta California during the Mexican period.

During the 1840s, land grants were made throughout the area. Cayetano Juarez was granted Rancho Tulucay just east of the present city of Napa. Juarez built two adobes on his rancho and moved his family to them from Sonoma in 1840. He was a native of California, and when he died in Napa in 1883, he was buried in the Tulocay (modern spelling) Cemetery on land he had donated to the City of Napa. Other early grantees included Nicolas Higuera, a portion of whose Rancho Entre Napa encompassed the present city of Napa; Salvador Vallejo, captain of the militia at Sonoma and brother of General Mariano Vallejo, who occupied the land north of Entre Napa along the Napa River; Jacob Leese, whose Rancho

Huichica spanned the distance between the Sonoma and Napa valleys; Julian Pope, whose grant included the present-day Pope Valley; Joseph Chiles, whose rancho encompassed the valley which bears his name; and José Berryessa, whose enormous grants included the Berryessa Valley and today's Lake Berryessa. Damaso Rodriguez and Ygnacio Berryessa were also given grants of land in the Napa Valley during this period.

Settling to the north of George Yount was Dr. Edward Turner Bale. Bale, an English physician, came to California in 1837. He soon built a reputation, not only as a man of medical competence, but also as one with a penchant for alcohol. Bale's temperament was erratic and he was often quarrelsome. Nevertheless, Dr. Bale's skill as a surgeon was of great value on the frontier and he was made surgeon-in-chief of the Mexican Army in Alta California. Bale had married Maria Ignacia Soberanes, a niece of General Mariano Vallejo and Salvador Vallejo, in 1839. In 1841 Bale became a citizen of Mexico, and through the influence of General Vallejo was granted most of the land in the Napa Valley north from Yount's Rancho Caymus. Present-day St. Helena and Calistoga both lie within the boundaries of the original grant to Bale.

Bale's relationship with the Vallejo family was not always pleasant. Salvador Vallejo had Bale flogged in Sonoma for alleged aspersions Bale had issued against Vallejo's character. Sometime later Bale retaliated by shooting Vallejo. One shot grazed Vallejo's neck and the other hit Cayetano Juarez, with whom Vallejo was walking. Bale was arrested, but was released by order of the governor who feared trouble with the English consul.

Edward Turner Bale is best known, however, for the Napa Valley landmark that bears his

© *Otto Hesemeyer 1967*

Dr. Edward Turner Bale completed construction of the Bale Grist Mill about 1846. Shown here as it appeared in the 1860s, the mill, with the help of its thirty-six-foot waterwheel, ground the Napa Valley's grain into flour. The mill's waterwheel was the largest in the West. Drawing by Otto Hesemeyer. Courtesy, Jack & Elayne Hesemeyer

name, the Bale Grist Mill. Bale had built a small gristmill and adobe dwelling on his Rancho Carne Humana (meaning human flesh) as early as 1840, but nothing as ambitious as the project he was about to undertake. Sometime between 1843 and 1845, Bale contracted with Ralph Kilburn to build a new gristmill. Kilburn did not complete the mill because he found the sluice was not sufficient to carry water to it. The remaining portion of the mill was completed by Thomas Kittleman in 1846 or 1847. When Bale's gristmill was completed, it had a twenty-foot overshot waterwheel (water entered from the top of the wheel). However, this wheel apparently did not provide enough power during the dry summers and was replaced in

Above: *In the late 1800s the profession of miller was very well respected, and Napa Valley millers were among the leading citizens of the community. Mr. Mecklenberg and Mr. Scott, two of the Bale Grist Mill's operators, are shown here about 1890 posing in the mill complex. Courtesy, Napa County Historical Society*

Facing page: *In nineteenth-century Napa Valley cattle were raised for the hide and tallow trade, the valley's most important economic activity in pre-Gold Rush California. This Charles Russell pen-and-ink drawing titled* The Hide Trade of Old California *depicts hides being transported to a ship for export. Courtesy, Amon Carter Museum, Fort Worth, Texas*

the early 1850s by the larger thirty-six-foot wheel that can be seen today. The Bale mill had the largest wooden waterwheel in the West. The wheel weighed five and a half tons and generated forty horsepower. According to early settlers, the noisy wooden cog gearing could be heard miles away. During this same period, Bale had Kilburn build a sawmill for him on the Napa River on the present site of the Charles Krug winery.

In 1848 Bale went off to the gold mines to search for the precious yellow metal. He returned to his rancho after a year's fruitless search and died there on October 9, 1849. Some say that Bale contracted a fever in the goldfields from which he never recovered. Others record that he died of a malignancy. Some say that he died as a result of his alcoholic habits. However, estimates of Edward Turner Bale generally place too much emphasis on his drinking. Actually he seems to have been a competent physician for his time. Nathan Spear, founder of a mule-powered gristmill in the village of Yerba Buena in the winter of 1839 to 1840, spoke highly of Bale's medical skill. Becoming ill of heart trouble in 1845, Spear moved to Bale's rancho to have the doctor's care. Moreover, Bale got along well with Napa Valley pioneers who built the mill or worked for him in its operation and was generous in his business dealings. He gave acres of his rancho to Florentine Kellogg in exchange for the iron work he did on the mill. In a larger perspective, credit should be given him for conceiving the mill and for being one of the pioneer industrialists of California. Bale Grist Mill State Historic Park, which includes the restored mill buildings, serves as a monument not only to Dr. Edward Turner Bale, but also to the rancho era he epitomized in the Napa Valley.

For Mexico the ranchos served as means to the settlement of the Napa Valley, and the land grant system facilitated that goal. Most ranchos were composed of grasslands of wild oats grazed by large herds of cattle. The cattle roamed at will, but were tended by the Indians who lived on the rancho. Cattle were raised for the lucrative hide and tallow trade that flourished throughout Mexican California. Wheat, the major crop grown on the ranchos, was cultivated by the Indians there. Unlike hides and

James Clyman settled in the Napa Valley on land he soon developed into a dairy and farm. A former mountain man, he had accompanied one of the first overland wagon trains to the West in 1845. This Smith & Elliott lithograph of Clyman's residence and farm dates from 1878. Courtesy, Napa County Historical Society

tallow, little of the wheat grown was exported. At first, mills such as Bale's and Yount's were custom mills and ground wheat only for local consumption. Later, when threshing machines replaced Indian labor and the California Gold Rush created an enormous demand for flour, growing and milling wheat would supplant hide processing as the Napa Valley's principle economic activity.

The romantic era of the Mexican rancho was to be relatively short-lived in the Napa Valley. American interest in the West, and particularly in California, was growing. The idea of Manifest Destiny, the theory that it was inevitable and necessary that the United States have its western boundary at the Pacific Ocean, seemed

to push settlers ever westward. Interest in California had already been aroused by fur traders and merchants, but now interest was growing.

The first overland migration of Americans to California left Independence, Missouri, in 1841. This was the Bidwell-Bartleson Party consisting of some sixty people. Several of these immigrants settled in the Napa Valley because George Yount vouched for them as desirable aliens to the Mexican authorities. Among these new settlers were Charles Hopper, Colonel Joseph B. Chiles, and the first woman to cross the Great Plains, Mrs. Nancy Kelsey.

Joseph Chiles and Charles Hopper were true frontiersmen. Hopper guided immigrant trains across the Sierras to California prior to settling in the Napa Valley. Joseph Chiles, with Joseph Walker, led his own party across the Great Plains to California. In 1844 Mariano Vallejo granted Rancho Catacula, known today as Chiles Valley, to Colonel Chiles.

Among the other pioneers who settled the Napa Valley in the 1840s was Colonel James

Clyman, who left an extensive journal. Clyman was born in Virginia in 1792 and moved to Ohio in 1812. During the War of 1812, Clyman served as a ranger and a spy on the north Ohio border. After the war, he surveyed lands in Indiana for the federal government and then enlisted in Governor William H. Ashley's 1823 expedition against the Arikara Indians. Clyman took part in the Black Hawk War of 1832, serving in the same company as Abraham Lincoln. After this war, Clyman moved farther west and navigated the Great Salt Lake in buffalo-hide boats. He was appointed a colonel in the U.S. Army, but resigned after two years. Clyman crossed the Plains with a company of immigrants bound for Oregon, where he left the party and journeyed to Napa in 1845. He returned east and came back across the plains to California, finally settling in the Napa Valley with his wife, Hannah. Clyman's exploits earned him national recognition, but he chose to spend the rest of his life on his fruit and dairy ranch in the Napa Valley, where he died in 1881 at the age of 89. James Clyman, along with his comrades Jedediah Smith, Jim Bridger, and Joseph Walker, epitomized the spirit of the American frontiersman.

The Napa Valley of the 1840s was quite different from today's lush vineyard-covered slopes and bottomlands, as several early accounts illustrate. James Clyman mentioned in his diary that in much of Napa County there were "wild oats as far as the eye could extend," and that the "mountains are litterly covered with deer and Bear." As plentiful as nature's storehouse may have seemed in the Napa Valley, James Clyman dispells much of that image in describing the area around Edward Turner Bale's house, which he said "looked desolate enough standing on a dry plane near a dry black volcanic mountain almost destitute of vegetation . . .

and about 10 or 12 Indians lying naked in the scorching sun finished the scenery of the rural domain."

The new immigrants from the East were to change this landscape. By the time that John Russell Bartlett traversed the Napa Valley as a commissioner with the United States and Mexican Boundary Commission in the 1850s, the valley had changed. He stated in his *Personal Narrative* that the "larger portion of Napa Valley was still in the state in which nature had left it, but had all been taken up by recent settlers, and was fast being brought into cultivation. A road had just been laid out through its centre, and . . . ploughs were cutting up the virgin soil in all directions."

Land in the Napa Valley for the overland pioneers was limited though, and by the late 1840s Mexican land grants covered virtually all of the productive soil. Some of the new settlers bought land, and some performed services in exchange for a parcel. Others became squatters.

Land ownership became a source of major conflict during this period, and this caused tensions to mount between the recent American immigrants and the Mexican grant-holders. California had become a neglected Mexican province. Its missions were secularized, causing the power of the Church to decline and further weaken Mexico's hold on its northern province. Texas had declared its independence from Mexico, a fact which was not overlooked by American settlers in California, and the idea of Manifest Destiny had been embraced by many of the new immigrants whose loyalties remained with the United States. It was inevitable that the tension over land ownership would serve as a catalyst for conflict. That conflict would come soon in the form of California's Bear Flag Rebellion, in which Napa Valley's new settlers would play a key part.

Napa Valley settler Peter Storm purportedly made the original bear flag that was raised in Sonoma in 1846. Storm is shown here about 1846 with his flag, which was modified to become the flag of California. Courtesy, Napa County Historical Society

Chapter 2

CONFLICT AND CHANGE

The United States government had become increasingly interested in California during the 1840s. Inadequate Mexican control of Alta California could have encouraged British seizure of it. The United States and England were already at odds over the Oregon Territory, and the U.S. did not want any further extension of European power in the Americas. With this in mind, the United States government sent John C. Frémont on several expeditions west. In the spring of 1846, while on the third of these expeditions, Frémont camped near Sutter's Fort (Sacramento). A large number of American settlers soon gathered at Frémont's camp for protection. They had become alarmed by the rumors that the Mexican government was about to forbid further immigration into California, and they were fearful of a confrontation. Frémont told them that he could not commit any act that might be considered hostile toward a nation at peace with the U.S. So the settlers decided to take matters into their own hands.

A group of twenty men under the leadership of Ezekiel Merritt left Frémont's camp on June 11, 1846, bound for Sonoma and determined to stage a revolt against Mexican rule. They crossed the hills between the Sacramento and Napa valleys during the night and arrived in the upper Napa Valley the next day. Messengers alerted the local settlers of the party's arrival, and the group grew to thirty-three in number, including Samuel and Benjamin Kelsy, John Grigsby, David Hudson, William Hargrave, Harrison Pierce, Elias Barnett, and Nathan Coombs, among others. They held a meeting at Bale's mill, and the next day the group entered Sonoma. The town was ungarrisoned at the time, so the party met no resistance as they captured Mariano and Salvador Vallejo. After Mariano Vallejo signed articles of capitulation, Napa Valley settlers Merritt and Grigsby and others escorted the prisoners back to Sutter's Fort. Californio and Napa Valley resident Cayetano Juarez attempted to rescue the Bear Flag prisoners, but was thwarted when Mariano Vallejo refused assistance. (Vallejo would later become a respected citizen of the new state of California and play an important role in the formation of the new state government.)

Meanwhile, in Sonoma the Mexican flag was hauled down and the flag of the Bear Flag Republic was run up. The republic was short-lived, however, as war soon broke out between the United States and Mexico. California was occupied by American forces, and a change of government took place. The Treaty of Guadalupe Hidalgo ended the Mexican War, and California became a territory of the United States. Though the Bear Flag Republic had been in existence less than sixty days and had extended over no more than forty miles of territory, it made a lasting contribution to California in giving it its state flag.

Throughout the 1840s migrations westward continued to take place. From May to July of 1846 some 2,000 immigrants plodded their way westward across the Great Plains. One of the immigrant caravans, the Donner Party, has ties to the Napa Valley's history.

The Donner Party began in much the same fashion as earlier groups. Outfitted with supplies, hopes, and dreams, they crossed the Mississippi River headed for California. Near Fort Hall, Idaho, a major stopping point on the trek west, the members of the Donner Party were warned by guides who had made the crossing, that they were starting out too late in the year and could become caught in the fierce Sierra snows. It is an irony of history that one of the individuals who pleaded with the leaders of the party was James Clyman. Clyman warned the Donners that they should not take the shortcut they were contemplating, but rather, should take the well-established trail. Clyman stated that it was "barely possible to get through if you follow it [the known route[and it may be impossible if you don't." Several members of the group now disagreed over which route to take, so the group split up. Reason P. Tucker and his family took the older route, while the Donners could see no reason not to try the new, shorter route which had been recently advertised. The Tuckers crossed the Sierra Nevada safely, and in the fall of 1846 arrived in California.

The Donners did not fare as well. The party became trapped in the heavy snowfall of the Sierras, and many perished. A few members of the Donner Party managed to get out of the mountains and they sent to Sutter's Fort for assistance. Reason Tucker was in charge of one of the relief parties, and personally managed to rescue some of the survivors of the Donner tragedy. Tucker cared for Sarah Graves Fosdick, who lost both her husband and her parents in the ordeal. When the Tucker family settled in the Napa Valley south of Calistoga, Fosdick was with them. She became the teacher in Napa County's first school, opened opposite the Bale Grist Mill. The Tucker family became influential community members.

Following the Bear Flag Rebellion and the initial influx of Americans, another event took place which would influence settlement in California and in the Napa Valley and again link the name of Napan James Clyman with destiny. On January 24, 1848, nine days before the end of the war with Mexico, James Marshall, who had come to California in 1845 with the Clyman-McMahon party, discovered gold in the tailrace of Sutter's sawmill near Coloma.

Thousands of newcomers flocked to California's goldfields in what was one of the largest mass migrations in world history. While many of the Napa Valley's residents left for the mines, most of her farmers stayed on their land. The Gold Rush created an enormous demand for flour, and the price of wheat skyrocketed. The valley's custom mills began to grind grain as rapidly as possible to meet the Gold Rush demand. Napa County became second only to Santa Clara County as the leading producer of wheat in California during this period.

As gold fever subsided, squatters settled everywhere, and the breakup of the large ranchos escalated. The treaty that ended the Mexican War had guaranteed Californians their liberty and property, but the Land Law Act of 1851 required all Californians to prove the validity

Reason P. Tucker came to the Napa Valley in 1846. He had originally been a member of the ill-fated Donner Party, but he and his family broke away from that group and safely arrived in California. Tucker was in charge of one of the relief parties that successfully rescued some of the survivors of the Donner tragedy. Courtesy, Napa County Historical Society

of their title to land grants. The long, costly process to prove title deprived many landowners of their holdings. One of the last remaining large grants of land was George Yount's Rancho Caymus. When Yount died in 1865, however, his will stipulated that his grant be split into fifty-acre parcels and sold off. After his death the town of Sebastopol was renamed Yountville in his honor, and a new era began in Napa Valley history.

An economic shift had occurred as land was fenced and cultivated, and the Napa Valley's future became centered around its agriculture. The forces of nature hastened this shift.

Prior to 1861 the land east of the new town of Napa (surveyed in early 1848) was a vast cattle range. In the winter of 1861 a heavy rainfall occurred, followed by weeks of extremely cold weather. Cattle were completely exterminated in some sections of the valley. Carcasses dotted the range, and owners had the hides stripped from the animals in order to salvage something from their losses. The severe winter of 1861 was followed by a great drought in the valley in 1863 to 1865. Due to a lack of grain with which to feed their cattle, ranchers were forced to sell their recently built-up herds. When the drought years ended, wheat was replanted and again became the valley's major crop. Cattle ranching and the associated hide and tallow trade, however, were never restored to their former economic importance.

As the land ownership patterns and the economy of the Napa Valley region changed, so did its political boundaries. In April 1849 General Bennett Riley was appointed military governor of California by President Polk. Governor Riley called for the election of delegates to hold a state constitutional convention. The convention met at Monterey and lasted six weeks. The outcome was a state constitution.

With an official constitution, one of the first duties of the legislature in 1849 was to divide the Territory of California into counties. The highly respected General Mariano Vallejo, a delegate to the constitutional convention, was chairman of the committee assigned this task. Napa was one of the original twenty-seven counties recommended by Vallejo's committee and formed by an act of the legislature.

The first election in Napa County was held in 1850 with the following individuals elected as the first county officers of the new government: Judge, John E. Starke; Coroner, Florentine E. Kellogg; Surveyor, J.E. Brown; Sheriff, N. McKinney; Treasurer, Ralph Kilburn. At the time the county was organized, a County Judge and two associates made up the governing body. On May 2, 1852, the legislature created a county board of supervisors to succeed the court as the body of the county government. On December 6, 1853, the first elected board of supervisors, consisting of John Hamilton, Jesse Whilton, and Florentine E. Kellogg, held their first meeting in the town of Napa.

As the county of Napa was forming, its communities were developing. The town of Napa City was founded by Nathan Coombs in 1847, and the townsite was surveyed by James M. Hudspeth. The adobe houses of Cayetano Juarez and Nicolas Higuera were the only buildings in the area at the time. The town began at the point where the Napa River was navigable at high tide, the Embarcadero. Harrison Pierce, a former miller at Bale's gristmill, built the first commercial structure in the new town. Pierce, as well as Nathan Coombs, had been a member of the Bear Flag Party mentioned earlier. After Pierce framed his new structure, Nicolas Higuera, the original land grant owner, discovered that Pierce had built it in the middle of what Coombs had laid out as

Main Street. Napa City seemed to be off to a good start with its first building erected in the middle of a major street! Pierce then moved his structure out of the street and to a new location, but he didn't immediately open it. Having heard of the discovery of gold in the Sierra foothills, Pierce left to search for the precious metal. He returned disillusioned from the mines a short time later and opened his new building as the Empire Saloon.

The first general store in Napa was built in 1848 by Joseph P. Thompson, followed closely by a second built by General Mariano Vallejo and his son-in-law, John Frisbie. That the town was hardly booming at this point was substantiated by the fact that John Trubody mowed most of the townsite in 1848 and sold the hay to the government. But before long Napa began to take shape with the construction of other stores, warehouses, and "many half-canvas structures held together by redwood shakes."

To cross the Napa River early residents had to ford it at low tide. But in 1848 ferry service was started and soon a toll bridge was built. Contributions from citizens eventually made it a free public bridge.

By 1851 a two-story structure was erected in the city. This building served as a church, courthouse, jail, and theater. A tax assessment of twenty-five cents per $100 value of real estate was levied on Napa citizens as payment for the temporary courthouse. Construction of a new courthouse was begun in 1856 after the growing citizenry expressed their dissatisfaction with the original. Soon after, a jail and jailhouse were completed. In 1864 large cracks appeared in the courthouse walls, and within a few years the building was condemned as unsafe. Since the county judge refused to conduct court in the building, and the public demanded a usable structure, a new courthouse was built in 1878. It still stands as part of the county office complex.

Napa had soon grown into a full-fledged town as a *Napa Register* 1868 editorial illustrates. "The stranger coming into our town after dark, now finds a generous gas light at nearly every street corner, and we can hardly

Above: *This circa 1910 photo of Rutherford was taken looking down Main Street, now State Highway 29. George Yount's granddaughter, Elizabeth, married Thomas Rutherford, and land upon which the town of Rutherford grew was her dowry. Photo by Turrill and Miller. Courtesy, The Society of California Pioneers*

Top: *St. Helena was founded by Englishman Henry Still in 1853 when he purchased 100 acres of land and offered a free lot to anyone who would open a business on his property. St. Helena was soon known as one of the most beautiful villages in the state. This turn-of-the-century Turrill and Miller photo shows St. Helena's Main Street. Courtesy, The Society of California Pioneers*

believe. . . that the Napa of today with its excellent and fine schools, churches and public buildings, its streets and shops lighted with gas, and its railroad facilities, to be the same hamlet of a half dozen years ago."

The town of Napa City was officially incorporated by a special act of the legislature in 1872, but was reincorporated on February 24, 1874, as the City of Napa. The town had grown from a mere 300 citizens in 1852 to

1,800 in 1870 and 3,730 in 1880.

In 1853 Englishman Henry Still purchased 100 acres of land upvalley from the town of Napa from his former countryman, Dr. Edward Turner Bale. Still opened a small store on the land and offered a free lot to anyone who would build and open a business on his property; and so, St. Helena became established. The new town soon boasted a blacksmith, livery stable, saddlery, tailor's shop, dry goods store, shoe store, doctor's office, hotel, and town hall. It was known as one of the most beautiful villages in the state. One contemporary account stated that, "for beauty of natural scenery, healthful climate, plain, honest, pleasant, western country folks, advantages commercial, political, social and religious, I am sure it cannot be excelled in the state."

Calistoga was developed as a resort in the 1860s by Samuel Brannan, and sported several cottages and a hotel. (More about Calistoga will be discussed in chapter five.)

In 1852 Napa County had a population of 2,110, "including 1,330 Indians." By 1880 the county had grown to over 13,000 inhabitants. Directly linked with the growth of the county

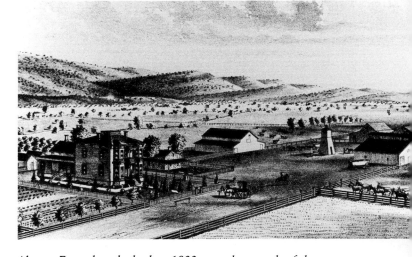

Above: *Even though the late 1800s saw the growth of the Napa Valley's communities, most of the county still remained agricultural and rural. Abraham Clark's 10,000-acre ranch in the Berryessa Valley, depicted here in 1878, was the largest in Napa County during this period. Lithograph by Smith and Elliott. Courtesy, Napa County Historical Society*

Top: *John Lawley's toll house was located on the Napa County side of Mount St. Helena. It continued as a private operation until 1922, when Napa and Lake counties purchased it for $10,000. As soon as the purchase price was recovered from the new public toll road, the State Highways Commission acquired it and opened it as State Highway 29, which today remains the main thoroughfare connecting Lake and Napa counties. Photo by Turrill and Miller. Courtesy, The Society of California Pioneers*

was the growth of various modes of transportation. Prior to 1850 people travelled throughout the county on horseback and trails crisscrossed the valley, connecting one rancho with another. However, as the population increased and agriculture developed, roads were needed, especially to facilitate the hauling of grain by wagon.

On October 7, 1851, the first county road was authorized by the Court of Sessions of Napa County. It extended down the center of the valley, but winter floods in 1852 rendered this road impassable. So a new route (now known as the Silverado Trail) was built on the eastern side of the Napa Valley, and by 1878 historian C.A. Menefee noted that, "the roads are everywhere greatly improved . . . the principal one from Napa City to Calistoga being heavily gravelled for eighteen miles to St. Helena."

In the second half of the nineteenth century, John Lawley applied for a permit to construct a toll road from Calistoga over Mount St. Helena to Lake County. Lawley owned a ranch in the Berryessa Valley, and, in 1866, after the crops were harvested, he took a crew of men to start building his toll road. He completed his road without the use of mechanized equipment. Lawley levied a toll on the freight wagons that supplied the mines and on the growing population that travelled between Lake and Napa counties. Lawley's toll road served for over fifty years, until it was finally purchased by Napa and Lake counties in 1922. It was designated as a public road sometime later, and portions of it are now designated as State Highway 29.

Bridges were also important to the development of transportation in nineteenth-century Napa County. The first bridges were made of wood, but the narrow Napa Valley with its wooded slopes allowed turbulent, debris-filled floodwaters to wreak havoc on every wooden bridge built. Then, in the late nineteenth cen-

tury, R.H. Pithie, a Scottish stonemason, settled in the upper Napa Valley and presented a plan to build a stone bridge to replace a damaged wooden structure over the Napa River from St. Helena's Pope Street to the Silverado Trail. When completed in 1894, the durable Pope Street Bridge became a model for those that would follow. Pithie received contracts for other bridges throughout the county. The most famous of the later bridges was the span in the Berryessa Valley of Napa County over Putah Creek, one of the chief water barriers of the area. The Putah Creek Bridge was the largest stone bridge west of the Rocky Mountains, and it became the "queen of the stone bridges." By the early twentieth century, Napa was known as the "county of stone bridges," with no fewer than sixty erected across the Napa River and its tributaries. Unfortunately, the Putah Creek Bridge is now under man-made Lake Berryessa, but Pithie's Pope Street Bridge still accommodates traffic and serves as a reminder of this earlier period of transportation in the valley.

As Napa County's roads and bridges improved, so did its forms of transportation. Stage lines connected various communities in the valley. One ran between Calistoga (at the head of the valley) and Napa City, and another connected Napa City with Benicia and its ferries to points on the bay. Bill Spiers of Calistoga owned a stage line to Lake County and

Right, top: *In the late nineteenth century, the county contracted for the construction of several stone bridges. The most famous of these was the Putah Creek bridge. Shown under construction about 1900, the bridge spanned Putah Creek, one of the county's chief water barriers. Courtesy, Napa County Historical Society*

Bottom: *When the Putah Creek bridge was completed, it was the largest stone bridge west of the Rocky Mountains and became known as the "Queen of Stone Bridges." By the early twentieth century, Napa County was known as the county of stone bridges with no fewer than sixty spanning the Napa River and its tributaries. Photo by Turrill and Miller. Courtesy, The Society of California Pioneers*

drove his own stages as well. His stages took over 14,000 people annually over the Lawley toll road. Clark Foss, who serviced not only the quicksilver mines, but also had a tourist route to the geysers, built a toll road to Knight's Valley north of the Napa Valley and charged one dollar per mile for his routes.

Overland transportation in early years had been discouraged by the notoriety of bandits who frequented several Napa County routes. Black Bart, perhaps the most infamous of these robbers, foiled capture throughout northern California as he raided Wells Fargo Express Company stages. He was finally imprisoned in 1883. Buck English, another highwayman, long evaded apprehension, but was captured in 1895. Several others made it their business to waylay the stages carrying miners' wages to Napa County's quicksilver mines. However, the era of the stage robber was relatively short-lived. In 1910 Napa Valley's stages came to an abrupt halt when motorized buses took over their routes.

Throughout the county's early years, water transportation was important. Water served as the only means of direct commercial linkage between the Napa Valley and the rest of California. It is unlikely that when Nathan Coombs laid out Napa City on the northern-most navigable portion of the Napa River, that he did so without knowledge of the importance of that transportation artery. The first known landing at the point of embarcation, the Embarcadero, in what would become Napa City, occurred in 1844 when the *Sacramento* landed. The first steamboat to navigate the river was the *Dolphin* in 1850. The *Dolphin*, powered by a small locomotive engine, had begun its trip in San Francisco.

Both freight, such as hay, lumber, and coal, and passengers were carried by the early vessels

Above: *Charles Boles, the notorious Black Bart, robbed Wells Fargo stages in Northern California and managed to avoid capture until the early 1880s. Outlaws like Boles discouraged overland travel in Napa County, making the county's creeks and rivers even more important transportation routes. Courtesy, Mercaldo Archives. From Cirker,* Dictionary of American Portraits, *Dover, 1967*

Facing page, top: *Stagecoach lines ran up and down Napa County during the 1880s and 1890s. Stages connected Calistoga at one end of the valley with Napa at the other. Stage lines also extended into Sonoma and Lake counties. The passenger stage shown in this circa 1905 Turrill and Miller photo is set to depart from the front of the Calistoga Hotel in Calistoga. Courtesy, The Society of California Pioneers*

Bottom: *William Spiers, one of Napa County's most colorful individuals, owned one of the largest stage companies in California. His six-horse stage, shown here in front of his Calistoga stable, traversed the Lawley toll road from Napa County to Lake County's resorts, carrying over 14,000 people annually. Photo by Turrill and Miller. Courtesy, The Society of California Pioneers*

that plied the Napa River. In 1852 a ferryboat was operating near Soscol, south of Napa, and a wharf was constructed to accommodate both the ferry and the Petaluma-to-Sacramento stage line which met it. As the town of Napa City grew and the valley became developed, the river traffic grew to meet this need. Grain and flour were the predominant commercial products shipped, but mercury flasks from the quicksilver mines and hides from the tannery were also loaded aboard the river vessels, thus illustrating the importance of this major form of transportation to Napa County. When the commercial agricultural basis of Napa County shifted from wheat to wine, so did the cargos of the steamers.

Large quantities of wine were shipped in puncheons (eighty-four-gallon casks). In 1879 one steamer had 100 puncheons of wine along with its cargo of lime, apples, sheep, and sewer pipe. One of the early crafts, the *Paul Pry,* was considered a fast steamer in 1859. It could make the San Francisco to Napa trip in three hours. The largest vessel to operate on the Napa River was the *Amelia,* owned by the California Steam Navigation Company. The *Amelia* was registered at close to 400 tons and was 147 feet long.

Top left: *The Napa River was not only a major transportation route, but also a place for pleasure boating.*

Top right: *The construction of the Napa Valley Railroad, which connected Calistoga and Napa, greatly aided commercial transportation in the county. The train, depicted in the foreground of this 1878 lithograph, traversed the length of the Napa Valley. It increased the ability to transport passengers and the valuable grain harvest. Also shown here are the residence and ranch of H.C. Parker. Lithograph by Smith and Elliott. Courtesy, Napa County Historical Society*

Bottom: *From 1898 to 1929 the Southern Pacific Railroad ran steam trains from Napa to Calistoga in the Napa Valley. The Calistoga Depot (shown here) served as the terminus of the line for passengers travelling to the community's resorts. In 1929 Southern Pacific replaced its passenger rail service with bus service. Photo by Turrill and Miller. Courtesy, The Society of California Pioneers*

The commercial importance of river traffic was not lost on chroniclers of the period. John Russell Bartlett wrote in the 1850s that: "A steamboat now runs to San Francisco, which will tend to populate rapidly this beautiful valley, and render the town of Napa the centre of one of the richest agricultural districts in the State." River commerce was important to Napa County until well into the twentieth century, when the more economical trucks replaced the steam vessel.

As important as the stage and steamer were to Napa County transportation, it also became evident that other forms of travel were necessary. As early as the 1860s the *Napa Register* stated that: "the need for some better means of transportation is apparent. Some of our county roads are in such shape that it takes a boat to navigate them, not a wagon." The development of a railroad system was an important transportation link in the Napa Valley's history.

The construction of the Napa Valley Railroad, which began in 1864, was intimately tied to the development of Calistoga as a resort. When completed, railroad lines connected Calistoga to Napa City, and steamers connected Napa City to San Francisco. The valley's grain shipments increased during this period partly due to these efficient transportation systems. In 1898 the valley's railroad lines became part of the Southern Pacific Railroad system, but in 1929, again due to the advent of the automobile, bus, and truck, the steam locomotive made its last round-trip upvalley. Southern Pacific had requested abandonment of the steam train line from the State Railroad Commission with the understanding that bus service would be substituted. On June 16, 1929, a new era of transportation began when Southern Pacific's bus service replaced its ferry and passenger rail service. Freight rail service continued until 1985

when a portion of the line was sold to a new group known as the Wine Train.

Outlasting the steam train was an electric railroad. The Vallejo, Benicia, and Napa Valley Railroad Company was incorporated in 1902 for the purpose of building an electric railroad from Benicia in Contra Costa County through Vallejo to Calistoga. In 1905 the electric railroad line opened between Napa and Vallejo, where it connected with steamboats to San Francisco. In 1911 the road was reincorporated as the San Francisco, Napa and Calistoga Railroad Company, which continued service until the 1940s.

Communication with Napa County greatly improved in 1858 when twelve citizens in Napa subscribed $100 each and paid for a telegraph line between Vallejo and Napa. In 1867 the

line was extended to Calistoga. For fifty cents, a message of ten words could be sent over the line. This telegraph system was transferred to the Western Union Telegraph Company in later years. The year 1883 brought the first telephone service to Napa.

Along with the major transportation and communication improvements of the late nineteenth century came utility service. The Napa City Gas Light Company was incorporated in 1867. The company built a gas works with a 10,000 cubic foot capacity. Gas was generated from coal and piped through condemned boiler tubes, which were utilized as street gas mains. The county board of supervisors ordered that street lamps be installed throughout Napa City, with the gas company receiving nine dollars per month for each lamp serviced. On September 1, 1867, Napa became the tenth city in California

Above: Bicycle shops, such as the Carrol Inman Cycle Shop in the city of Napa, did a booming sales business as well as providing for the servicing of cycles. As soon as the automobile became affordable to the general public, the bicycle, like the horse, was no longer an indispensible means of travel. Photo by Andrew P. Hill. Courtesy, Napa County Historical Society

Facing page, top: The electric railroad, or Interurban as it was known, changed the features of the communities through which it ran. The Third and Suscol intersection in Napa is shown in this circa 1910 photo. Notice the interurban tacks and the overhead electric lines that powered the train. Photo by Turrill and Miller. Courtesy, The Society of California Pioneers

Bottom: In 1908 the electric Vallejo, Benicia, and Napa Valley Railroad began running through St. Helena. The line ran down Main Street, today a part of State Highway 29 through the Napa Valley. The overhead electric line powered the railroad engine, seen on the tracks in the distance. Photo by Turrill and Miller. Courtesy, The Society of California Pioneers

Throughout the nineteenth century Napa County increased in population, and by 1900 the area had over 16,000 inhabitants. With this population came not only industry, but also the services provided by retail outlets such as drugstores, clothing stores, markets, and stationers. Abe Strauss' clothing store (above) and the New York Meat Market (above right) in Napa were typical turn-of-the-century establishments. Courtesy, Napa County Historical Society

to receive gas lighting. A "lamplighter," usually a boy on horseback, lit each lamp at the end of each day and put them out each morning. In December 1887 electric service was installed in Napa City.

In 1869 the Napa and Vallejo Water Systems was incorporated, but the system failed to become established. After several more attempts to establish a water system, the Napa City Water Company was founded in 1883 by Samuel Holden to supply water to the city. Water was obtained from a dam on the Napa River and directed into a pumping plant from which it entered the town's distribution system. Wells later augmented the system, but by 1922 the supply had become inadequate. In the twentieth century an inadequate water supply has become a major problem not only for the City of

Napa, but also for the entire Napa Valley.

With the increase in transportation and utility systems, the Napa Valley continued to increase in population, reaching 16,451 people by 1900. With this growth came industry such as planing mills, manufacturing companies, a tannery, glove factory, carriage factories, and many others reflecting the needs of a growing area.

Throughout the mid-nineteenth century, wheat was Napa County's primary crop and was responsible for the valley's wealth. Well over ten percent of all grain in the United States came from Napa County. The increased efficiency brought about by better roads and transportation systems not only made it easier to get grain to nationwide markets, but also easier to develop, produce, and ship other agricultural products.

Other than wheat, fruit was the major crop grown in the valley. William Huston Nash, known as the "first importer of fruit trees into California," came overland in 1846. Nashville, Tennessee, had been named for his family and built on his uncle's property. William Nash was at first a member of the ill-fated Donner Party,

but split off from the group and arrived safely in the Napa Valley by another route. He planted peach trees and, during the inflationary period created by the Gold Rush in 1849, sold 100 peaches for $100! In 1853 he imported English walnuts from England and experimented with grafting and budding. His farm was so successful that he later counseled other farmers on the soil preparation, planting, and marketing of fruit trees. He became well known and respected throughout California.

Orchards were planted throughout the Napa region, and by the 1860s 150,000 trees, mostly apple and peach, were growing in the valley. By the 1880s olives and prunes also became important tree crops. In 1890, 300,000 fruit trees were planted and in 1910 over 500,000 were growing. By the turn of the century, prunes became the dominant crop in the Napa Valley. The grape also became a major crop during this period of increasing agricultural diversity.

Pressure to diversify was partly caused by a declining price on wheat brought about by overproduction. While wheat continued into the twentieth century as an important county crop, the Bale Grist Mill symbolized the change in agriculture in the Napa Valley when, in 1879, it ground grain for the last time. And, in that year, the dreaded plant infestation, phylloxera, hit vineyards in France and created a new market for California grapes.

Above: *In the 1850s wheat harvesting had advanced from Indian labor utilizing wild horses to mechanical machinery pulled by domestic horses. By the 1880s modern equipment such as that illustrated in this 1878 lithograph of one of Napa County's ranches increased harvesting efficiency. At one point in time, well over 10 percent of all grain in the United States came from Napa County. Courtesy, Napa County Historical Society*

Top: *Early wheat harvesting, as depicted in this circa 1880 photo, was an arduous task. After the Napa Valley's wheat was cut, it was piled in an open area and either baled for feed, as shown here, or winnowed. Winnowing was the process of separating the grain from the chaff (discard material). The grain was then piled on horse-drawn wagons and taken to the closest mill. Courtesy, Denzil and Jennie Verardo*

This stylized depiction of an early Napa Valley wine press shows how much manual labor was still involved after mechanization improved on the Spanish method of wine production. A Roman press similar to that in the illustration is located at the Nichellini Winery and saw limited use until the 1950s. Drawing by Otto Hesemeyer. Courtesy, Jack and Elayne Hesemeyer

Chapter 3

THE CRUSH IS ON

Grapevines were not a new sight in the Napa Valley in the 1800s. Early reports tell of wild grapes growing on the hillsides long

before the Mexican ranchos were established. Apparently the Indians did not use these wild grapes for fermentation, probably

because their bitter taste, small size, and large seed rendered them practically useless in comparison with other native fruit.

Spanish missionaries brought grapevines with them to California. Father Junipero Serra planted the first non-native vines in

Alta California in San Diego in 1769. By the late 1700s production of wine at the missions seems to have exceeded the

padres' sacramental and medicinal needs, and a small trade in wines had begun. By the 1820s enough wine and brandy were being produced locally to cause the Spanish governor to first tax imported wines, and then, in 1824, to forbid their importation. Though the ban was later lifted, duties on imported wine and brandy remained high, probably as protection for local producers.

During the rancho period in California, grape growing and wine production were almost completely limited to the missions. When these were secularized by the Mexican government in 1834, wine production fell into neglect. However, in neighboring Sonoma Valley, General Mariano Vallejo kept up both the production and the quality of his wine. He continued to export the beverage and traded with the Russians at Fort Ross as well as with the Mexicans.

In this early period, black "mission" grapes were the only variety available. Descriptions of the wine produced from these grapes ranged from laudatory praise to "passable" to "sour, unpalatable stuff which served its purpose." This discrepancy could be credited partly to the method used to produce the wine in the early 1800s. At the time there were no crushers and few, if any, available winepresses, so Indian labor was utilized. L. L. Palmer, an historian of the Napa Valley writing in the 1880s, described the Spanish method of wine production: "They literally trod the wine press. The grapes were put into troughs made for the purpose, and the Indians then trod upon them with their bare feet, until the whole mass was a pumace. This was then removed and placed in cow skins, so suspended that they would retain the greatest possible amount of it. These were their fermenting tanks, and here the pumace remained during that process. When this was accomplished, a hole was cut in the skin and they drew the wine off and put it into casks." Most of the wine produced in this manner was used locally and very little was seen as a commercial product.

With the discovery of gold near Coloma and the ensuing rush to find the precious metal came new markets for manufactured and agricultural products, especially wine. By the mid-1850s, convinced that wine making could prove profitable, J.M. Pachett purchased land in the Napa Valley upon which a small vineyard had been planted. On this property near Napa City Pachett planted a large number of additional vines. In 1858 he contracted with a young Prussian, Charles Krug, to produce a vintage using a small cider press. The endeavor was apparently successful, producing 1,200 gallons of wine. It represented the first production of wine in the Napa Valley by other than the Spanish method.

Krug was not a novice at wine making when he embarked on this innovative venture for Pachett. Born near Cassel, Prussia in 1825 and educated at the University of Marburg, Charles Krug first immigrated to Philadelphia when he was twenty-two, returning to his native country the next year to take part in an attempted overthrow of the reactionary Prussian parliament. The revolt failed, and Krug was imprisoned for nine months before he was able to escape and eventually make his way back to Philadelphia. He became a U.S. citizen and in 1852 moved to California. Before settling on his eventual profession of viticulturist, Krug was a German-language newspaper editor, a failed farmer in San Mateo, a worker in a private gold-refining establishment, and a clerk for the United States Mint.

By 1858 he had saved enough to purchase twenty acres of property in the Sonoma Valley from Count Agoston Haraszthy. During the next two years Krug planted vines on his property, although no mention is made of wine being produced there. It may be assumed that Krug was under the tutelage of Agoston Haraszthy

Charles Krug's cellars and a portion of his vineyards are depicted in this 1878 lithograph by Smith and Elliott. At the time this lithograph was made, Krug had the largest vineyard in Napa County with 112 of his 800 acres planted in vines. His 350,000-gallon capacity wine cellar was also the county's largest at the time. From Smith & Elliott, Illustrations of Napa County, California, *1878*

while in Sonoma, and that they were not strangers before Krug's move to that county. Haraszthy, known by some as the father of California viticulture, may be one of the most disputed figures in California wine-making history. Like Krug, Haraszthy was an immigrant, arriving from Hungary in 1840. His involvements both in Hungary and in the United States appear even more colorful than those of Krug and include several allegations of fraud and embezzlement. Nevertheless, Haraszthy did invest a great deal of his own time and money to bring European varieties of grapevines to California as well as to promote California wines both in

Above: *The Beringer Brothers wine cellar and residence stood among ninety-seven acres of land, twenty-eight of which were vineyards, in 1878. At the time, the* St. Helena Star *called the Beringer Brothers wine cellar "the most handsomely finished of any in the valley, and for solidity of build and completeness of appointments can have no superior anywhere." From Smith & Elliott,* Illustrations of Napa County, California, *1878*

Top: *The prosperous Beringer Brothers posed in front of their distillery in 1894. Jacob is in a plaid vest on the left of the arch while Frederick (with his thumbs hooked in his vest) is to his left. Young Charles, who would become president of the company, stands between them. Courtesy, Napa County Historical Society*

this country and abroad. He seems to have had a positive influence on his young friend, Krug, and they apparently had mutual respect for their viticultural involvements.

In 1860, after having produced Pachett's wine and having become familiar with the Napa Valley, Charles Krug sold his Sonoma property. In December of that year he married Dr. E.T. Bale's daughter Caroline and established his new family on the land north of St. Helena which had been her dowry. They immediately began to plant grapes.

At about the same time a few miles to the south, Dr. George B. Crane was beginning to experiment with cuttings obtained from Haraszthy on steeper, rockier soil than was formerly thought to be usable for grapevines.

Krug and Crane were not alone in their viticultural pioneering in the Napa Valley. By the mid-1860s, there were over 1,000 acres of valley land planted in grapes. The nearly thirty vineyards were composed of about 750,000 vines. In addition, there were some fifty vintners who had become prominent in the valley.

The 1870s marked a period of tremendous growth in the Napa Valley wine industry. By 1875 local viticultural clubs were organizing, including the St. Helena Club with Charles Krug as its first president. These groups acted as networks for exchange of information on methods of grape and wine production and as lobbyists for the wine industry.

Charles Krug had by this time constructed the largest wine cellar in the Napa Valley with a 250,000-gallon capacity. He had also become known as an excellent wine maker and a premier brandy producer.

Downvalley, Jacob Beringer used the earnings from his position as Krug's cellar foreman to purchase ninety-seven acres and, with his brother Frederick, established the Beringer Brothers winery in 1877. Their cellar was described as "the most handsomely finished of any of the valley and for solidity of build and completeness of appointments can have no superior anywhere." Dug into the hillside by Chinese laborers and walled with stone, it represented an architectural as well as a masonry feat.

The Beringer brothers had come from a wine-making background in Mainz, Germany,

Gustave Niebaum's Inglenook Winery is depicted here as it appeared in 1883. Niebaum, who earned his fortune as a partner in the Alaska Commercial Company, settled near Rutherford. In 1889 his Inglenook wines took awards for overall excellence at the Paris Exposition, and they continued to do so until Niebaum's death in 1908. Inglenook wines still signify quality. Drawing by Otto Hesemeyer. Courtesy, Jack and Elayne Hesemeyer

T.L. Grigsby's three-story white and gray lava stone wine cellar was the largest in the valley in 1878. A distillery for making brandy stood about sixty feet south of the 112-foot by 58-foot cellar. From Smith & Elliott, Illustrations of Napa County, California, *1878*

to New York, where they had a wine-marketing operation. Moved by a desire for their own vineyards and winery, they came to the Napa Valley. The brothers' first vintage was produced in 1879, and for nearly 100 years the winery would remain in family hands. Frederick Beringer had the now-famous Rhine House built in front of their cellars. The seventeen-room mansion is said to have been a duplicate of the family home in Germany. It reflected the prosperity that was beginning to be enjoyed by Napa Valley vineyardists.

In addition to the fine cellars that local vintners like Krug, the Beringers, Jacob Schram, and Gustave Niebaum were erecting and the abundant, well-received vintages they produced, Napa Valley viticulturists received a boost from

Above: *The plant louse phylloxera devastated the valley's vineyards in the late 1800s. After a louse-resistant rootstock was found, entire vineyards had to be replanted. All work was done by hand during the 1890s and replanting could prove an arduous task. Some growers combined vineyards with orchards to prevent total devastation from occurring again. Courtesy, John and Gladys Wichels*

Left: *Twin disasters of depression and phylloxera stilled activity in many Napa Valley wineries in the late 1800s. Wine presses, like this one at the Jacob Grimm Cellar on Healdsburg Road west of Calistoga, remained idle as wine prices plummeted. Photo by Turrill and Miller. Courtesy, The Society of California Pioneers*

the outbreak of phylloxera in the French vineyards in the late 1870s. Phylloxera is a plant louse that attacks the vine and can eventually cause the plant to wither and die. By 1879 French vineyards were devastated. (Phylloxera had been observed in Sonoma Valley vineyards as early as 1873, but it was not perceived as a threat.) Grape production was increasing to the point of overproduction and the reduced French competition produced new markets for California wines. During the 1870s grape growing and wine production employed more workers than any other branch of California farming.

While new markets were stimulating wine production in California, other forces were at work which would soon shake the industry to its foundations. The worst depression ever to occur in American history had begun in 1873. Its effects were not immediate upon the wine industry, but by 1876 a recession was being felt in California wine sales. In addition, an internal revenue tax was placed on brandy, which would further impact the vintners' situation. In 1877 the wine industry reached an all-time low with wine selling for ten to fifteen cents a gallon and grapes for two to ten dollars per ton. By the late 1870s and early 1880s overproduction, a depressed economy, and poor quality wine spelled disaster for some Napa Valley viticulturists, including Charles Krug.

Krug's vineyards and cellar faced receivership in June 1885, at which time he listed some $236,000 in liabilities and assets of only $181,000 in Superior Court insolvency proceedings. His property was placed in a trust administered by his friend Charles Moffitt of San Francisco, but Charles Krug was not able to regain either his winery or his solvency before his death in 1891. That proved a sad and undeserved ending for a talented, respected pioneer Napa vintner.

Even the boomlet produced by the vineyard destruction in France and increased markets for Napa Valley wines were not enough to save many of the financially troubled vineyardists, especially with the onslaught of the next disaster poised to strike. Phylloxera, a boon while destroying French competition, was soon to mark the end of an era of wine production in the Napa Valley.

Beginning in the cooler, moister growing areas near the Bay, by 1893 the phylloxera infestation had seriously affected half of the vineyards in the Napa Valley and mildly affected most others. Within two years wine production fell from about 5,000,000 gallons (1890) to 2,000,000 gallons (1892). Meanwhile, the price for grapes had fallen from twenty-four dollars per ton in 1884 to eight dollars per ton in 1893.

As tragic a situation as it may have seemed, a great deal of good eventually resulted from the devastation. Mission variety grapes were virtually eliminated, and the overproduction that had plagued growers was checked so that decent prices could be demanded and received for their grapes and wine. A native, eastern United States grapevine was found which was resistant to phylloxera. By grafting varietal vines to this root stock, an excellent, louse-resistant grapevine could be produced. The disaster also brought about the formation of the State Board of Viticultural Commissioners in April 1880, a move that the industry had long sought. These commissioners, representing the seven districts in the state, were experienced vineyardists who

Above: *State Senator Seneca Ewer, owner of this winery, was active locally as a viticulturist and served as founding vice president of the St. Helena Viticultural Club in 1875. The F.S. Ewer Winery in Rutherford was sold to Georges de Latour in 1915 and became Beaulieu Winery. Photo by Turrill and Miller. Courtesy, Denzil and Jennie Verardo*

Right: *John C. Weinberger's Cellar near Lodi Lane was built in 1876 of red lava rock. It had one story underground, a second story to receive grapes at ground level, and a third for storage above. Here Weinberger developed grape syrup, which he apparently marketed for several years. Courtesy, John and Gladys Wichels*

could pass along information and advice to growers and could be instrumental in improving the quality of grapes and wine being produced.

By the mid-1890s wine in California was beginning to be reestablished as an important agricultural industry. Improved varieties of grapes were being grown, and along with innovations in the wine-making process, these changes were producing increasingly superior vintages. Napa

Above: *The Napa Fruit Company maintained extensive fruit-drying yards well into the twentieth century. In the late 1890s, many vineyardists dug up their phylloxera-damaged grapevines and replanted fruit trees. Prunes were especially popular in the Yountville and Napa City area. Courtesy, Napa County Historical Society*

Top: *Tiburcio Parrott had olives planted on his estate near St. Helena in the 1880s. Under the supervision of Joseph Callizo, Villa Parrott produced fine wines as well as 1,100 gallons of olive oil annually. In the 1980s the estate became the home of television's "Falcon Crest" vineyards. Photograph by Turrill and Miller. Courtesy, The Society of California Pioneers*

Valley wines were being honored in world-class competition and labels such as Niebaum's *Inglenook* and Jacob Schram's *Schramsburg* became synonomous with high quality.

Other vineyardists, having faced depression, grape overproduction, and phylloxera began to question the wisdom of their crops. French prunes were introduced, especially in the Yountville area, and by 1891, 160 tons of prunes were produced. Within a few decades, prunes became the dominant crop in the area between Napa and Yountville. Orchard crops of all kinds were attempted, and in 1889 olive trees were introduced and olive presses developed. By 1909 there were about 500,000 fruit and nut trees in the valley.

Still, viticulture remained the dominant agricultural activity in the valley in the late 1800s. In order to profitably keep up with the demand for Napa wines, cooperatives were being established. These companies would take the grapes from small vineyards and produce their wine. Since virtually no bank considered wine as collateral for loans, smaller producers were forced,

Built in the 1880s by William Bourne, Greystone was the largest stone winery in the world. Charles Carpy added it to the California Wine Association's holdings in 1894. After passing through several other hands and years of neglect, Greystone was purchased by the Christian Brothers in 1950. Pictured here circa 1900 is the entrance to Greystone. Photograph by Turrill and Miller. Courtesy, The Society of California Pioneers

by financial circumstances, to sell their grapes in order to raise the capital to produce the next year's crop, rather than cellar them as wine for later sale. Selling to a wine cooperative was often the only practical alternative. One such cooperative venture involved Napan Charles Carpy.

Born in France, Carpy eventually settled in Napa where he became a partner in the Uncle Sam Cellar. Located in Napa City on the banks of the Napa River, this brick establishment housed a half-million gallon capacity wine cellar operation as well as a 500-gallon

Above: *While mechanization had modernized early-1900 wineries, many tasks, such as unloading grapes, had to be performed by hand. Some vintners still feel that manual handling causes less harm to the grape and that it is worth the added costs. In 1900 there was no alternative. Photo by Turrill and Miller. Courtesy, The Society of California Pioneers*

Top: *Turn-of-the-century winery operations utilized horse-drawn wagons to transport grapes to the wineries. Roads were yet to be paved, but progress was beginning to be apparent. Photo by Turrill and Miller. Courtesy, The Society of California Pioneers*

distillery and a vinegar factory. Wine was transferred from here to San Francisco by boat. Carpy also owned cellars in San Francisco, which were built on opposite sides of the street with an underground pipe connecting them. In 1894 he purchased the defunct Greystone Cellars near St. Helena and later that year put all of his holdings into the newly formed California Wine Association. Charles Carpy became president of the San Francisco-based CWA, which had an almost overwhelming influence on

Although the 1906 earthquake caused $40,000 worth of damage in Napa, citizens quickly organized to help relieve the "suffering and want in San Francisco and Santa Rosa." Courtesy, Napa County Historical Society

prices and quality of California wine for the next two decades.

Wine making seems to have become a pleasant experience in the Napa Valley in the early 1900s. Napa wines continued to grow in reputation and markets and with few exceptions, the valley began the new century on a positive note.

Once again, however, nature stepped in to remind wine producers of her fickleness. The great earthquake of April 18, 1906, caused serious losses in Napa County both to commercial and viticultural establishments. But the destruction in the valley was nothing compared with that in San Francisco. The California Wine

Association alone lost over nine million gallons of wine. San Francisco had by that time become California's center for shipping, trading, and cellaring wines; so the losses were monumental.

Once again viticulturists picked themselves up and began to rebuild. And, once again, storm clouds began gathering, but the threat this time was not from nature. For several years there had been debate, often highly emotional, over the effects of alcoholic beverages on human morals. Local prohibition movements began to gain followers and momentum, and while most of the discussion involved hard liquor, wine was often included as a villain. As the debate increased, so did grape acreage and wine production. Viticulture was becoming a stronger, more lucrative industry employing growing numbers of workers. While wine was still a luxury for most Americans, its consumption and appreciation were on the rise.

Then at 12:01 a.m. on January 17, 1920, the Eighteenth Amendment to the United States Constitution went into effect, prohibiting the manufacture, transportation, or sale of intoxicating liquors. Viticulturists had fought hard to have wine excluded from the earliest legislation, but even the support of President Woodrow Wilson was insufficient for its exclusion. For most wineries in the Napa Valley Prohibition was a death blow, while a few were more fortunate. Viticulturists were allowed to produce limited amounts of wine for medicinal or sacramental purposes, and among those who survived were the Christian Brothers. A lay religious teaching order of the Roman Catholic Church, the Christian Brothers moved their wine-making operation from Martinez, California, to Mont La Salle in the Napa Valley in 1932. They had begun producing wine in 1882 for sacramental purposes and by 1887 found

themselves in the wine business. Seventy years later their Mont La Salle Vineyards was incorporated.

The Eighteenth Amendment allowed individuals to produce 200 gallons of wine per year for personal use, and the Napa Valley had the grapes with which to make it. Grape prices rose to $125 per ton for some varieties, and boxcar shipments of grapes increased as Prohibition dragged on. Acreage planted in grapes was actually increased after the initial impact of Prohibition subsided. A different type of grape was now in demand. Fine wine grapes were replaced with thicker-skinned, deeper-colored grapes that held up better during the long rail shipments.

By the late 1920s prices paid for grape juice had begun to decline, and when Prohibition was finally repealed in April 1933 the country was in the midst of the Great Depression. Wine, as a luxury item, was doomed to wait for recovery until the Depression and the ensuing World War II were memories. The wine industry, reborn in the 1950s and 1960s, was destined to be very different from its nineteenth-century predecessor.

By the end of World War II, the world had changed, and so had the Napa Valley. Recovery from the Great Depression and the ensuing global conflict began to signal the opportunity for growth and prosperity in the county. By the early 1960s the Napa Valley had regained its prominence as *the* American wine-producing region. Established firms such as the Beringer Winery, Inglenook, and the Christian Brothers were soon joined by new vintners, who were producing wines of recognized quality. The Mondavi family had purchased the Charles Krug winery in the late 1940s and was restoring its earlier reputation. By the late 1960s, Robert Mondavi had begun to establish himself as a premier vintner with his own winery downvalley

in Rutherford. The Carpy family was again involved in wine production, this time at Freemark Abbey. Others like Joseph Heitz, Fred McCrea, Hans Kornell, Jack Davies, and Louis Martini were setting benchmarks to be attempted by newer vintners. By the mid-1970s there were again over fifty wineries in operation in the valley, and a new marketing technique had been established—tasting rooms.

In order to allow the public to recognize just how fine a product they were creating, wineries opened their doors for tours and free wine tasting. The postwar romance with the automobile was enhanced by such inviting opportunities for new experiences and free entertainment. Travellers began to flock to the Napa Valley. At one point it was estimated that tourists visited the valley in numbers second only to those visiting Disneyland. In 1963 alone over 500,000 people visited Napa Valley wineries.

At about the same time that travellers "discovered" Napa Valley wineries, so did large corporations. Outside companies began to purchase the once family-owned wineries. The first large winery to change hands was Inglenook, which was sold to United Vintners by Gustave Niebaum's grandnephew, John Daniel, Jr., in the early 1960s. During the 1960s and 1970s title to many of the valley's wineries changed hands, some several times.

There were also cooperative wine-producing efforts being utilized during this period. A 1961 newspaper advertisement lauded one such venture by announcing:

Some vintners were able to survive Prohibition through the sale of wines for medicinal or sacramental purposes. The Christian Brothers were able to buy this Mont LaSalle winery in 1932 and relocate to Napa from Martinez through careful planning and profits from the sale of their sacramental wines. Courtesy, John and Gladys Wichels

We Salute Our Partners in Progress The Members, Officers and Directors of the Napa Valley Cooperative Winery and the St. Helena Grape Growers Coop Winery whose fine wines are produced exclusively for national marketing by the E & J Gallo Winery under our long-term marketing arrangments

The 1970s also saw what may prove to be a peak in the establishment of small, specialized wineries. Dozens of winemakers left service with large vintners to create their own unique style and character in both their wines and in their wineries. Grgich Hills, Rutherford Vintners, Robert Pecota Winery, and Markham are just a few of this new type of Napa Valley winery. By the beginning of the 1980s, there were more than seventy wineries operating in the valley and most offered tasting and tours.

In the 1980s, in response to increasingly sophisticated tastes and to the increasing value of some vintages, a few wineries in the valley began to offer premium wine tasting for a charge. And a new pastime may have been added to the visitors' growing list of activities. Since wine has become an increasingly popular beverage, especially among the young to middle-age group, the position of the valley as a wine producer seems fairly assured for some time.

This 1899 photo affords a rare look at the inside of a Napa schoolhouse, the South Primary School. Courtesy, Napa County Historical Society

Chapter 4

SPIRIT, MIND, AND VOICE

The spirit and character of any community are embodied in its institutions. Judicial and educational; humanitarian and religious; those represented by literary or artistic genius; all of Napa Valley's institutions are an integral part of its history.

Judicially, the *alcalde* system of civil government was in effect in the valley when the treaty ending the Mexican War conveyed California to the United States. General Riley, California's seventh American military governor, kept the Mexican system of government since the occupied territory was not yet a state of the Union. Lawlessness was increasing in the territory due to the massive influx of people seeking gold, and some order had to be imposed. In 1849 General Riley divided California

Above: *Over 90,000 bricks were used to build the Napa County Courthouse. Constructed in 1878 at a cost of $50,990, the courthouse was an architectural symbol of justice in Napa County. Courtesy, Napa County Historical Society*

Facing page: *The pride of a nineteenth-century fire department was its foreman and his trumpet. The Napa fire department was organized in April 1859 as the Pioneer Engine Company. Photo by Brayton. Courtesy, Napa County Historical Society*

into ten districts with an alcalde governing each. Under the laws of the Republic of Mexico the alcalde performed all legislative, executive, and judicial functions within a community. It was the alcalde who enforced both civil and criminal laws and could render judgments in those matters. In territorial California the alcalde functioned as the court of the first instance and the military governor acted as the appellate court. Ralph Kilburn, one of the Napa Valley's early pioneers, was appointed alcalde of the Sonoma district, which included the Napa Valley.

The California Constitution of 1849 provided that, "the judicial power of the State shall be vested in a Supreme Court, in district courts, in county courts, and in justices of the peace." When California became a state and the counties were formed, this new judicial system began to function. Justice courts inherited the alcaldes' jurisdiction, and the Supreme Court took over the military governor's role as an appellate court. County courts were organized with the district court exercising jurisdiction over several counties.

Justice courts were established in Napa County in each township. In 1852 the board of supervisors had created the three townships of Napa, Yount, and Hot Springs. The Knox township was added in 1873, and the St. Helena township was created in 1903, bringing the number to five. In 1930 the county was reorganized into three townships: Napa, St. Helena, and Calistoga.

The salary of a justice of the peace in Napa County was originally based on the fees collected by him in the performance of his official functions, but in 1883 fixed salaries were set. The job of justice of the peace was not an easy one as witnessed by the fact that in 1851 one of the first justices, J.A. Sellars of Napa, was stabbed to death in the performance of his duties.

One sensational early court case brought attention to Napa County. In 1856 Edward McGowan and James Casey were arrested as suspects in the murder of James King. All three were from San Francisco, where the murder was committed. Casey was lynched by San Francisco vigilantes, who then sought to capture McGowan. McGowan, who fled, turned himself in in Sacramento. On a change of venue, Napa County was selected for Edward McGowan's

Top: *From the 1850s to the early 1900s, private, one-room schoolhouses provided education for Napa County's rural population. The one-room Lodi School (shown here in 1888) was located on Lodi Lane between Calistoga and St. Helena. Courtesy, John and Gladys Wichels*

Above: *The Central School was Napa City's first eight-year grammar school. Built in 1868 at a cost of $17,000, the Central School served the community until well into the twentieth century. Courtesy, The Society of California Pioneers*

A woman teacher's salary at the turn of the century was approximately seventy dollars a month. Working in schoolhouses such as these located in Calistoga, teachers were very respected and honored members of the community. The buildings shown were typical of those that slowly replaced the rural one-room schools. Courtesy, Napa County Historical Society

trial. McGowan was at first permitted to stay in the Napa Hotel under the custody of the sheriff, but was moved to the county jail prior to the trial. Since McGowan was the sole occupant of Napa's new jail, he was given freedom to roam about it. He was also furnished with the best food, wines, and cigars from a local Napa restaurant. McGowan became popular, and actually admired, during his stay in Napa City. While the trial took place, Napa was crowded with reporters and visitors from San Francisco awaiting the outcome. At the completion of the trail, the jury acquitted Edward McGowan after deliberating for ten minutes!

In addition to organizing the court system, the legislature of 1850 also created the office of constable. A constable exercised law enforcement authority within the township in which he was elected. The sheriff was responsible for the remainder of the county's law enforcement.

As the judicial system in Napa County was growing and maturing, so was the educational system. In 1849 Sarah Graves Fosdick (a Donner Party survivor) opened the first school in the Napa Valley. Her private school, located near Bale's gristmill, was comprised of little more than a shelter. It was only the second such private school in California. William H. Nash soon erected a wooden building to serve as a proper schoolhouse for the children.

Before long, several one-room schoolhouses were built throughout Napa County and served the rural population well. These were private schools for the most part and they lacked lighting, running water, and most conveniences. But since few children could attend public school due to the need for their labor at home, this system filled a valuable educational niche in Napa County. Eventually there were about fifty one-room schools in the county.

Construction of the first non-private school in the county was financed by public subscription in 1855. However, the first true eight-year grammer school, the Central School, was not built until 1868 in Napa City. Central School was a large two-story structure which was constructed at a cost of $17,000 raised by a local tax. By 1872 Napa County had thirty-seven schools with over 2,000 children and nearly fifty teachers. Male teachers in 1872 earned seventy-seven dollars and fifty-eight cents a month while females averaged sixty-seven dollars and ten cents.

As additional grammar schools were constructed throughout the area, the need for a public high school was recognized. In 1893 the first high school in the county, located in a Presbyterian Church, was established in St. Helena. A private college-preparatory school, the Oak Mound School, had opened in Napa City in 1872, but it closed in 1897 when the students moved to the newly constructed Napa High School. In 1923 the county's third high school opened in Calistoga.

The Napa Collegiate Institute, Napa Ladies' Seminary, and Napa Business College were private schools of higher education which had opened their doors in the nineteenth century. The Napa Collegiate Institute was actually a forerunner of the University of the Pacific. The Institute was established in 1860 on a five-acre campus with a four-story main building. Money for the building was raised by $100 public subscriptions. During its first two years, the Institute changed hands twice. In 1862 the property was acquired by a group of Napans, who selected a president for the Institute and ran it under an informal agreement with the Methodist Church. In 1870 the California Conference of the Methodist Episcopal Church took over the

school.

During this period the Methodist Church was also running the University of the Pacific in San Jose. In 1896, due to the substantial financial commitment required to maintain two similar institutions, the Church closed its Napa campus. The University of the Pacific was moved to Stockton, and is today still nominally supported by the Methodist Church.

Nineteenth-century course offerings at institutions such as the Napa Ladies' Seminary and the Napa Collegiate Institute included mathematics, English, Latin, French, Italian, natural science, music, and painting. The Napa Collegiate Institute also had "mental and moral science" as a primary part of its curriculum.

Above: *In 1902 Napa's first public library building opened. Known as the Goodman Library, the facility was named after Carrie A. and George E. Goodman, who donated the land and building to the citizens of Napa City. Today the Goodman Library building is preserved as the main office, archives, and museum of the Napa County Historical Society. Courtesy, Napa County Historical Society*

Left: *Pictured is the chapel of the Christian Brothers School at Mont La Salle in Napa.*

Two other parochial education institutions were also established in the Napa Valley, both of which are still important today. Pacific Union College in Angwin was founded by the Seventh-day Adventists, and the Novitiate at Mont La Salle was founded by the Christian Brothers.

The Brothers of the Christian Schools, the Christian Brothers, opened a novitiate (training school) at Martinez, California, in 1879 and in 1932 moved their school to Mont La Salle in the Napa Valley. When in 1957 the Christian Brothers' Mont La Salle Vineyards was incorporated, the profits from their premium winery were used by the De La Salle Institute, the Brothers' educational and religious corporation, throughout California.

One public school of higher education, the Napa Junior College, was founded in the city of Napa in 1942 and today is part of the California Community College System.

The growth of libraries in Napa County coincided with educational development. The private Napa Library Association opened a library in Napa City in 1870 with 1,000 volumes. On May 2, 1901, the public Goodman Library opened. George E. Goodman had given property to the City of Napa for a public library. The original Goodman Library building serves

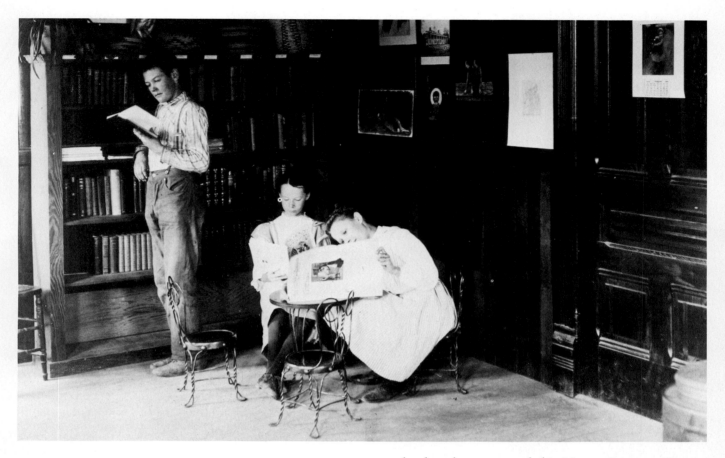

Above: *The St. Helena Library, which opened its doors in 1894, was constructed with Carnegie funds. A newer facility was built in the 1970s to meet the community's expanding needs and to house the famous St. Helena Wine Library Courtesy, The Society of California Pioneers*

Top: *The Calistoga Free Public Library opened in 1902. The children's corner, shown in this circa 1906 photograph, was always popular with that community's youth. Courtesy, California State Library*

as the headquarters of the Napa County Historical Society.

The Goodman Brothers, James and George, were extremely influential early Napa Valley settlers. They had opened the first bank in Napa City. George Goodman was also elected treasurer of Napa County in 1861 and held the position for nine years, as well as holding the position of trustee of both the Napa Collegiate Institute and the Presbyterian Church. James was one of the original directors of the Napa Valley Railroad Company, and the Napa City Gas Light Company.

The St. Helena Library and the Calistoga Free Public Library opened their doors in 1894 and 1902 respectively. The county library system was established in 1916 as the Napa County Free Library and serviced those portions of the county which did not have a city library. The

Above: *Construction of the first Catholic churches in the Napa Valley took place in Napa City in 1858, in St. Helena in 1866, and in Calistoga in 1892. Prior to the erection of these churches, a Catholic priest came from the Sonoma Mission and conducted mass in a Napa boardinghouse parlor. Shown here is the second St. Helena Catholic Church, built in 1890 as a replacement for the first which was destroyed by fire. The stone used for the structure was quarried locally. Courtesy, The Society of California Pioneers*

Left: *The White Church, shown here about 1890 and long unused, was the first actual church building erected in the Napa Valley. Built in 1853, the structure was named after Asa White, the Methodist minister who preached there. A few years later in San Francisco, White began construction of California's first Methodist church. Courtesy, Napa County Historical Society*

Napa City-County Library was organized in 1963, when the City and County of Napa agreed to merge their public libraries.

During the mid-nineteenth century, the Napa County Courthouse served as a gathering place for Protestant religious services whenever a minister came to Napa City. The first known regular minister to preach in Napa was the Methodist Reverend Samuel Simonds in 1857.

On November 13, 1853, the first actual church building was erected by settlers in the Napa Valley. It was a small pine structure named after its Methodist minister, Asa White. White was born in Vermont in 1797, and at the age of sixteen studied for the Methodist ministry in New York. In 1847 he made the trek westward across the plains to Oregon. In 1849, after gold was discovered, White moved to San Francisco where his Methodist ministry became well known.

While in San Francisco, White began construction of California's first Methodist church, which was completed in 1850. White was also one of the original donors to the California Wesleyan College, founded by the Methodists in 1851. In 1853 Asa White made his first appearance in the Napa Valley and preached his first sermon on lands owned by his friend, Florentine Kellogg, today the site of Bothe-Napa Valley State Park. The White Church was constructed there soon after.

White passed away in 1873 in Calistoga leaving behind as a fitting memorial the establishment of the first churches in Oregon City, San Francisco, Arcata, and Kelseyville, as well as

Churches sprang up throughout the Napa Valley in the mid- to late nineteenth century. Whether Presbyterian or Methodist, Catholic or Russian Orthodox, all denominations played an important historical role in meeting the growing community's spiritual needs. The Calistoga churches shown here were typical of such nineteenth-century structures. Courtesy, The Society of California Pioneers

the first church in the Napa Valley.

Other Methodist churches were built in Napa in 1858, in St. Helena in 1867, and in Calistoga in 1869. In 1867 the African Methodist Church was established to accommodate black

The St. Helena Sanitarium, opened in 1878 by a member of the Seventh Day Adventist Church, began one of the first training schools for nurses in California and earned a reputation as one of the best institutions of its class. Today the sanitarium is known as the St. Helena Hospital and Health Center. Courtesy, John and Gladys Wichels

Methodists. Prior to that time blacks met in a predominantly white Methodist church.

During this same period, a Catholic priest from the Sonoma mission would conduct mass in a Napa boardinghouse parlor. The first Catholic church in Napa County was built on Main Street in Napa City in 1858, followed by one in St. Helena in 1866 and Calistoga in 1892.

Nathan Coombs, who founded the town of Napa City, donated land for the Napa Methodist Church and later donated the land for the First Presbyterian Church of Napa (1874) and the Seventh Day Adventist Church of Napa (1873).

Since 1812, when Fort Ross was founded, the California Russian community has main-tained its Orthodox Church traditions. The Russian Orthodox Church in Calistoga serves one of the largest Russian communities in the state.

Other denominations too numerous to mention established churches or houses of worship in Napa County in the nineteenth and early twentieth centuries, and all have historically influenced the religious direction of the area. The early dates of church establishment show that houses of worship were important institutions to the early settlers of Napa County.

After the growth of institutions to care for the area's spiritual needs, came those facilities related to physical and mental health. In 1878 the St. Helena Sanitarium, located on the side of Napa County's Howell Mountain, opened its doors. Founded by W.A. Pratt, a member of the Seventh Day Adventist Church, as the Rural Health Retreat, the sanitarium stressed natural healing. In 1891 the sanitarium started one of the first training schools for nurses in California, and in 1914 a new five-story building was erected. A 1926 advertisement for the St. Helena Sanitarium called it, "the largest and best equipped medical and surgical institution of its class west of the Rocky Mountains." The twentieth century also saw the term hospital replace sanitarium. Continued growth and modernization have taken place since that time.

The first hospital in the city of Napa opened its doors in 1910. Founded by three medical doctors, the hospital was named after Dr. Benjamin Shurtleff, a local physician. Shurtleff was

Top: *The Napa State Asylum for the Insane was completed in 1876 at a cost of $1,500,000. As massive as the structure was, however, it soon became overcrowded. The asylum was built to accommodate 500, but in 1880 over 800 patients were housed in the institution. By 1881 even the attic had to be used for patients, and many of the mentally ill were discharged. Photo by Boon Fly. Courtesy, Napa County Historical Society*

Above: *This early Napa street scene illustrates the dominance of the Napa State Asylum for the Insane (background, center) on the area's landscape. Today the grounds of the former insane asylum are part of Napa State Hospital, and the former asylum building itself no longer exists. Courtesy, Napa County Historical Society*

one of the individuals who witnessed the first public surgical operation at which ether was used as an anesthetic at the Massachusetts State Hospital in Boston in 1846.

In 1918 a second hospital, the Francis Hospital, was constructed in Napa, and two years later the Shurtleff and the Francis hospitals were replaced by the new Victory Hospital. The Victory Hospital was renamed the Victory Memorial Hospital in 1946 when it became a non-profit community care facility. In 1958 the Queen of the Valley Hospital replaced the Victory Memorial Hospital, whose facilities had become inadequate.

The California Veteran's Home in Yountville began when the Grand Army of the Republic's (GAR) San Francisco chapter expressed concern over the lack of available care for disabled soldiers. In 1877 the GAR established a committee to study the situation. From their recommendations, the Veteran's Home Association was incorporated in 1881. A fund-raising campaign was begun, land near Yountville was purchased, and a building was constructed. In 1884, when the Veterans' Home opened, facilities included a kitchen and dining room, living quarters, sick wards, offices, and a chapel.

In 1885 the California Legislature appropriated $150 per person annually for those housed in the Veterans' Home as a supplement to the Home Association's fund-raising activities. In 1897 the State of California took over the property and the administration of the Veterans' Home. In 1932 a hospital was built as part of the complex. The Veterans' Home remains one of Napa County's important institutions, providing care for the state's disabled veterans.

The mentally ill in California were originally housed on a ship anchored in San Francisco Bay. An asylum was constructed in 1850 in Stockton, but became overcrowded by the mid-1860s. In 1872 a site for a second asylum was selected on 208 acres of land purchased in Napa from Cayetano Juarez and T.H. Thompson. A year later construction began on the Napa State Asylum for the Insane. Work stoppages and fund shortages delayed completion, and political charges of extravagant expenditures hampered appropriations. When completed at a cost of $1,500,000, the asylum housed 600 patients and was self-contained. The building and grounds had a laundry, bakery, its own water supply, ward facilities, dining rooms, libraries, a lumberyard, and a mortuary. The building was even lighted with coal gas manufactured on the premises.

The asylum was to be managed by a board of trustees appointed by the governor. In 1876 it was finally ready to accept patients. Contemporary views expressed sympathy for the "insane" as documented in 1893 in *Overland Monthly*. The *Monthly* commented that the Napa Insane Asylum represented "one of the finest of these public institutions in the United States." It was also seen, however, as a "sepulchre of living dead, a monument to ruined hopes and saddened lives."

In 1924 the California Legislature established the Department of Institutions and consolidated mental and correctional institutions under the one agency. The Napa State Asylum for the Insane was renamed Napa State Hospital in that same year. The departments of Health and Corrections were later formed from the Department of Institutions with the Napa State Hospital organized under the Department of Mental Health.

In 1985 Napa State Hospital was one of Napa County's single largest employers with a staff of some 2,500 individuals.

The spirit, mind, and voice of a community

Napa County Reporter.

OFFICIAL PAPER OF NAPA COUNTY.

PUBLISHED EVERY SATURDAY,

AT NAPA CITY, CAL.

BY

W. F. HENNING.

IN POLITICS DEMOCRATIC,

But Devoted Unceasingly to the Local interests of the County.

SUBSCRIPTIONS:

$4 Per Year.. In Advance.
To Clubs of Six or More............................$3 Per Year.

☞ Special attention given to Job Work and the advertising department.

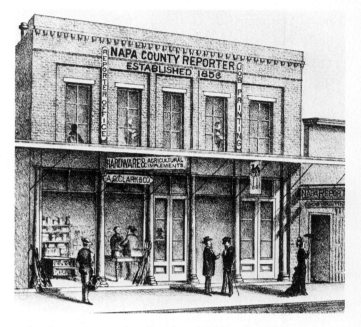

Above: *The* Napa County Reporter *was founded as the first newspaper in the county on July 4, 1856. This advertisement from the* Napa County Directory *dates from 1871. Courtesy, Napa County Historical Society*

Above, right: *The* Reporter *office was located over A.G. Clark and Company when this lithograph was printed in 1878. At the time, George W. Gift was the publisher and editor of the paper. From Smith and Elliott,* Illustrations of Napa County, California, *1878*

are not only embodied in its institutions, but also in its press and in its ability to foster creative genius. The free press in Napa County has both chronicled institutional growth and provided a window to the past as the voice of the community.

The Napa *Reporter* was founded as the first newspaper in Napa County on July 4, 1856. Issued on an irregular basis, after its first year the paper had fewer than twenty subscribers. In 1857 it was expanded and published on a regular schedule. After several changes in ownership, the paper finally began to flourish. At first the *Reporter* was apolitical, but by the 1860s it had taken a Democratic outlook and vehemently opposed the administration of

Abraham Lincoln. In the 1870s the *Reporter* was enlarged, its printing facilities were modernized, and machinery was converted to steam power. No less than eight other newspapers also sprang up in Napa City during this period including the Napa *Weekly Herald,* the *Napa Sun,* the *Napa Register,* the *Daily Advertiser,* and the *Pacific Echo.*

The *Pacific Echo* was published primarily to oppose the policies of the Lincoln administration and support the Confederate viewpoint. It ceased publication in 1865 with Abraham Lincoln's assassination.

Only the *Napa Register,* which was founded in 1863 and which had been an advocate of the Republican Party, survived as a newspaper into the 1980s. As the largest circulation newspaper in Napa County, the *Register* serves as the primary means of local news communication in the valley.

The *Calistogan* has been published in Calistoga since 1877, and the *St. Helena Star* has served that community since 1874.

One of the most sensational events to hit the early press concerned Eadweard Muybridge,

Above: *Eadweard Muybridge, known as the "Father of the Motion Picture," earned the label when he successfully adapted motion photographs to a projection machine. Muybridge was tried for murder in Napa after killing his wife's lover, but he was acquitted. Courtesy, Denzil and Jennie Verardo*

Above, left: *The* St. Helena Star *has been published since 1874, making it one of the county's oldest newspapers. This lithograph illustrates the* Star *office in 1878. At the time it was the only newspaper in the county occupying its own building. Courtesy, Napa County Historical Society*

later known as the "father of the motion picture." Muybridge was born in 1830 in England and immigrated to the United States in 1852. At first he settled into the book business in San Francisco, but soon began a study of photography which would make him one of the most notable photographers of his day.

In 1872 Muybridge became friendly with Leland Stanford, and with Stanford's support began photographic experiments of objects in motion. In 1879, at Stanford's house, Muybridge adapted drawings made from his photographs to a projection machine, the zoopraxiscope, and began the first exhibition of motion pictures on a screen. From the zoopraxiscope, the modern cinematograph evolved. Muybridge eventually took over 30,000 motion photographs before his death in England in 1904.

Ironically, the event which sparked headlines for Muybridge in Napa's press did not involve his motion experiments. It was his trial.

In 1871 Eadweard Muybridge married Flora Stone. Flora gave birth to a son in 1874, but Muybridge discovered the father was not he, but rather, an acquaintance, Harry Larkyns. A contemporary newspaper account stated that, "the remainder of the story may be condensed into a few sentences: Muybridge was away from home frequently and bestowed more care on business than domestic affairs. Mrs. Muybridge was vivacious and young enough to be his daughter; Harry Larkyns was gay, dashing and handsome, and having permission to escort Mrs. Muybridge to the theatre, he did not neglect the opportunity and abused it."

Muybridge, who was living in San Francisco, took the ferry to Vallejo and caught the train up to the Napa Valley to Calistoga, where Larkyns was residing. Muybridge finally tracked Larkyns to the Yellow Jacket Mine in Napa

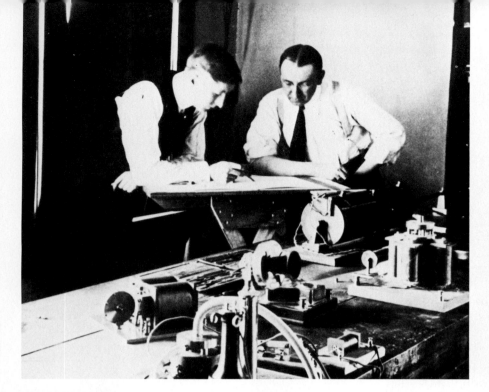

Above: *Peter Jensen and Edwin Pridham, shown in their Napa laboratory in 1915, accidentally invented the first loudspeaker while working on an improved telephone receiver. They startled Napa residents when their roof-mounted loudspeaker played music that carried for two miles. Courtesy, Magnavox Government and Electronics Company*

Above, right: *Robert Louis Stevenson was the valley's most important literary figure. Arriving there in 1880, Stevenson resided in an abandoned miner's cabin on Mount St. Helena's slopes. Although his stay was short, Stevenson immortalized the area with the publication of the* Silverado Squatters *in 1883. The book chronicled Stevenson's time in the valley. Etching by H. Coit from photo by Lloyd Osbourne*

County, confronted him, and shot and killed him. Muybridge was arrested and transported to Napa for trial. He stated to the press that he had "loved the woman with all my heart and soul, and the revelation of her infidelity was a cruel, prostrating blow . . . I feel I was justified in what I did."

The trial was headline news. Napa had not seen such excitement since the town's citizens left for the Gold Rush. The defense pointed out that Eadweard Muybridge did what was normal and what others would have done, while the prosecution had the fact of murder itself. After deliberating a relatively short time, the jury brought in the verdict of not guilty. Eadweard Muybridge was acquitted and the crowd assembled outside the courthouse applauded. Muybridge left the Napa Valley bound for a photographic survey of Central America,

and one of California's most sensational trials had ended.

The voice of the press was not the only one that made an impact on the populace of the Napa Valley. A loud voice was quite literally heard in 1915. In the spring of that year two inventors, Edwin S. Pridham and Peter L. Jensen, were working in the city of Napa on an improvement of the telephone receiver. During their experimentation, they created a device that gave a loud broadcast of their voices. Pridham and Jensen had accidentally invented the first loudspeaker.

Pridham and Jensen now wanted to test the distance at which their new loudspeaker could be heard, so they mounted it on the roof of their Napa laboratory and talked and played music into a transmitter. The residents of Napa were startled by the sound of the great voice and music. The voice bellowed, "Can you hear me?" and was audible within a radius of two miles. A posse formed in the town to search out the sound as many members of the populace were understandably frightened. The posse converged upon the sound from different points and finally surrounded the laboratory of the Commercial Wireless and Development Company. The world's first loudspeaker had been located, and Napa's frightened inhabitants could be put at ease.

The laboratory established in Napa by Peter Jensen and Edwin Pridham as the Commercial Wireless and Development Company was the beginning of the Magnavox Company. Magnavox is Latin for "great voice," which it proved to be when first demonstrated in the city of Napa in 1915.

A history of the spirit, minds, and voices of the Napa Valley would be incomplete without mention of the individual who left the greatest literary impact on the area, Robert Louis Stevenson.

Stevenson was born in Edinburgh, Scotland, in 1850. When he was twenty-five, tuberculosis forced him to leave Scotland in search of a more arid climate. In Paris he met an American, Fanny Osborne, his future wife. Stevenson followed her to San Francisco and they were married there. Still plagued by the chronic illness that afflicted him, Stevenson was advised by his doctor to leave San Francisco for a warm dry climate.

Almost penniless during this period, the Stevensons could not afford accommodations. Friends of Fanny and Robert Louis Stevenson mentioned Mount St. Helena at the upper end of the Napa Valley because they knew the mountain contained several abandoned miners' cabins. Thus Calistoga became a destination for the Stevensons. On May 22, 1880, the couple arrived in the valley.

While seeking a place to reside, the newlyweds visited Jacob Schram. Schram was one of the Napa Valley's first vintners, and Robert Louis Stevenson immortalized him in the *Silverado Squatters*. Stevenson sampled Schram's wine and stated that Jacob Schram, "followed every sip and read my face with proud anxiety . . . I tasted every variety and shade of Schramberger." Stevenson commented that California wine was still in the experimental stages, but in the future would come the time when, "the wine is bottled poetry."

Shortly after visiting the Schrams, the Stevensons took up residence in an abandoned cabin near the deserted mine of Silverado. Located on the side of Mount St. Helena, Silverado was above the damp fog that plagued Stevenson. While residing at Silverado, Stevenson would walk down to Lawley's Toll House to mingle with travellers bound for Lake County and occasionally even walk to Calistoga.

Though Robert Louis Stevenson's stay in the Napa Valley was not long, and he soon returned to his native Scotland, the impact of the area on his writing is well documented. Not only did Stevenson immortalize the Napa Valley with the publication of the *Silverado Squatters* in 1883, but he also recalled Mount St. Helena in *Treasure Island,* perhaps his most famous work. First published in book form in 1883, the latter novel contains a description of the island and its peaks. Stevenson wrote that, "gray-colored woods covered a large part of the surface," and that Treasure Island contained, "many tall trees of the pine family, outtopping the others—some singly, some in clumps . . . The hills ran up clear above the vegetation in spires of naked rock. All were strangely shaped, and the Spyglass, which was by three or four hundred feet the tallest on the island, was . . . suddenly cut off at the top like a pedestal to put a statue on." This described Mount St. Helena in virtually every respect. Today Mount St. Helena is fittingly preserved, virtually unspoiled, as Robert Louis Stevenson Memorial State Park.

Silverado Squatters and *Treasure Island* show the influence of the Napa Valley on Stevenson, and with their publication Robert Louis Stevenson made a lasting literary impact on the spirit, mind, and voice of the area.

Most of the work in the nineteenth century was hard and often monotonous, but early valley residents knew how to celebrate holidays. This Fourth of July parade in St. Helena in 1885 featured marching units and carriages down uncompleted Main Street. Photo by Lewelling. Courtesy, California Historical Society, San Francisco

Chapter 5

ROCKCRUSHERS, RESORTS, "HEATHENS," AND A "HERETIC"

The Silverado that Robert Louis Stevenson so eloquently spoke of was, in 1874 and 1875, the largest producing silver mine in Napa County. By the late 1800s, mining had become an important economic activity in the valley. It all began with a silver rush in 1858 centered in the Mount St. Helena area which "involved every unemployed man from Soscol to Calistoga" as prospectors. Little silver of marketable quality was found then, but in January 1860, while on a hunting trip, A.J. Bailey and J. Cyrus discovered cinnabar in the Mayacamas range northwest of Calistoga. Shortly afterward, a ledge of cinnabar was found in Knights Valley.

Cinnabar ore reduced by heating in a retort produces

an end product of mercury, or, as it is often called, quicksilver. As glamorous and exciting as prospecting for gold or silver may have seemed, it was cinnabar that proved to hold the real mineral wealth of Napa County. Quicksilver was much in demand in the late 1800s as it was used to recover gold and silver from ores by amalgamation, in the manufacture of fulminating caps for explosives, and in drugs and paints. From 1864 until 1903, Napa County was one of California's leading quicksilver producers.

The first company organized to extract cinnabar was the Phoenix Mining Company, formed in 1861. By 1871 the Phoenix produced 73,440 pounds or $50,673 worth of mercury per season. By the end of World War I, when a decline in mercury prices forced closure of most mines, a total of $15,200,000 worth of quicksilver or mercury had been produced in Napa County. Quicksilver mines, such as the Aetna, the Knoxville, the Oat Hill, and the Red Hill, whose names remain as landmarks, represented an important contribution to the county's economy and at least partial satisfaction for those afflicted with "mining fever."

During the same period that quicksilver mining was reaching a peak, there was renewed conviction that Napa County contained silver. In 1872 Alexander Badham, nephew of Samuel Brannan, staked a claim to the Monitor Ledge on the southeastern slope of Mount St. Helena. Around this claim, owned by the newly organized Calistoga Mining Company, grew the settlement of Silverado City. At one point, Silverado had 1,500 citizens, a two-story silver stamp mill, several saloons, as many as eight businesses, and a hotel. Built in 1874, the Silverado Hotel was referred to as the "upper boarding house" in Robert Louis Stevenson's *Silverado Squatters*. During boom times, $2,000

worth of silver bullion per day was extracted from the mines in and around this claim. Then, in 1875, the ledge ran out. Apparently due to faulting, the silver ledge was cut off and its continuation has never been found. Soon after, the mine was abandoned, the buildings disassembled and moved to other, more productive claims, and Silverado was left to be immortalized as a ghost town by a young novelist and his new bride.

Another silver strike was made in the Palisades area east of Calistoga. With the mill that had been transported in pieces from Silverado down the Lawley toll road's twelve percent grade, the Palisades Mine began operation in 1888. During the next four years it produced $306,250 worth of silver. It has been estimated that $1,000,000 worth of silver was mined in Napa County, creating not only material wealth, but also a rich and romantic legacy of mining history for the valley.

While most of California seemed to be off to the mines of the Mother Lode and later the Comstock of Nevada, the majority of Napa Valley residents stayed in the valley, bent on achieving their wealth through hard work and laying a solid foundation for productive industry in the county. Early on, these industrial endeavors included leather tanning, garment and glove production, dairying, and lumber processing.

Napa City is still headquarters and home to one of the county's first manufacturing plants. F.A. Sawyer established the Sawyer Tanning Company in Napa in 1869 as a wool pullery. He had realized that the local butchers were throwing away sheep pelts with the wool in place and, seizing the opportunity, began to remove the wool for profit. A year later, his father, B.F. Sawyer, came to join him after having sold his successful Newport, New Hampshire, tannery. Together the Sawyers decided to

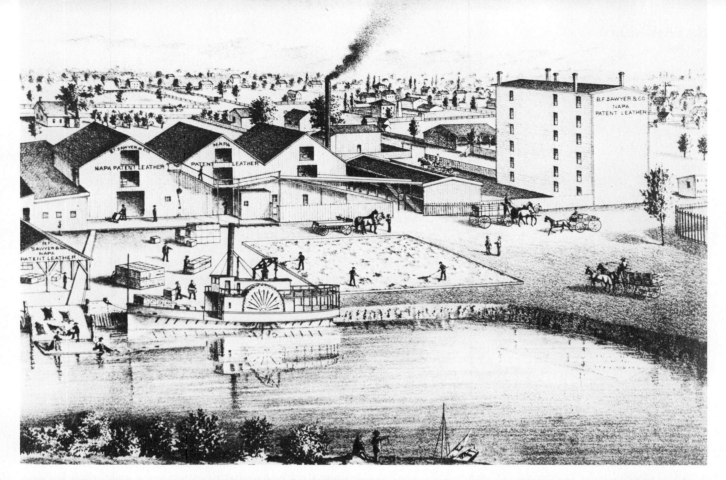

Top: *The Sawyer Wool Pullery and Tannery was one of the earliest industries in the valley. Specializing originally in wool production and sheep skin tanning, the company later added cow-leather processing and made "NAPA" leather famous. Lithograph by Smith and Elliott. Courtesy, Napa County Historical Society*

Above: *Employees gathered in 1919 to celebrate the fiftieth anniversary of the Sawyer Tanning Company. Sawyer was a family-owned business and many of the workers had learned their jobs from their fathers who had also worked at Sawyer. Courtesy, Napa County Historical Society*

Above: Labor unrest in several Bay cities may have been a catalyst for business relocation to Napa during the late nineteenth century. The only local involvement with any of the unrest seems to have been Company H, which contained Napans and was sent to Oakland to protect Southern Pacific Railroad property during a violent employee strike in 1895. Courtesy, Napa County Historical Society

Top: This 1908 St. Helena baseball team was playing long before the Sawyer Tannery developed a new leather for baseball gloves. Its successors have benefited from that development. Photo by Porter. Courtesy, Napa County Historical Society

build a facility to complete the process on the sheep skins by tanning them locally, and the Sawyer Tanning Company was born. So successful was this company that "NAPA Leathers" came to signify the finest quality in leather, and European competitors began stamping their products with that trade name with little regard to international copyrights.

The Sawyer Tannery was responsible for several innovations in hide tanning, among those being Napatan Waterproof Leather, which, between 1909 and 1918, was used extensively in shoes; and Napa Patent Leather, which was used widely in the United States and exported to seventy foreign countries. The Sawyer Tannery had been the first tannery west of Chicago to produce patent leather when the process was begun in 1926. In 1927 the tannery developed a chrome-tanned leather which proved perfect for softball covers. This was followed by a leather developed for baseball gloves, a washable garment of calfskin, and a specially tanned split for use in welders' gloves. By 1939 the Sawyer Tanning Company was the largest tannery west of the Mississippi. The company continues to produce the finest quality leather and has maintained the deserved reputation of Napa Leather.

Over the years the Sawyer Tannery was joined by other tanners in the Napa area. In 1874 Thomas Bain established the Napa City Tannery, which by 1912 was described as "an extended and profitable business." After that time, however, no mention is made of the company. In 1946 the Manasee family, which had been involved in the Sawyer Tanning Company for many years, founded Calnap.

As adjuncts to the tanning business, two other early industries in the valley involved the production of gloves and shoes. The Napa Glove Factory was organized in 1903 with

R. Raymond as president. About the same time, E.H. Raymond purchased the foundry building in St. Helena from Taylor, Duckworth and Company and converted it to glove production. It seems that labor unrest in San Francisco had forced some factory owners to seek more amicable surroundings. In 1926, having worked for the Raymond firm for twenty-six years, Louis Ferrogiaro established his Ferro Glove Company in Napa. In 1928 Napa's Keig Shoe Factory was "turning out a good first class work shoe, also a semi-dress shoe and a sporting shoe" and was said to be "the only maker of this kind of shoe on the Pacific Coast."

In 1919 the Rough Rider Clothing Manufacturer had begun in a loft in San Francisco, and by 1939 it had moved to Napa, expanded its operations, and had become "one of the largest makers of pants and sports coats in the West." In 1954 a manufacturing facility was established on Oak Street in Napa to accompany the Soscol Avenue Rough Rider facility built in 1936. The Cameron Shirt Factory became part

of Rough Rider in 1955. The shirt company had been a part of the valley's manufacturing community for more than thirty years and had at one time another plant in Santa Rosa. By 1970 Rough Rider was one of the four largest private industries in the valley. By 1980, however, it had closed its Napa operations entirely due mainly to the high cost of domestic labor and a changing climate in the garment industry.

Napa City was and is the hub of industrial activity in the valley. In 1928 the Napa City Directory listed six basic advantages that Napa possessed for industry, most of which still hold true today. They were: "accessability of raw materials, low priced power in abundance, labor

Above: *This 1896 photo of Chinese children in front of the Joss House in Napa's Chinatown was labelled, "California Products: Native Sons of the Golden West." Courtesy, Napa County Historical Society*

Top: *Many hotels and boardinghouses were centers for social events. Courtesy, Napa County Historical Society*

supplied with ideal living conditions, the transportation facilities already mentioned (Carquinez Bridge and the highway system), and an ever-increasing market for manufactured products . . . Because of exceptionally advantageous climatic conditions, every day here is an ideal day for factory employees. The manufacturer finds labor here at least 25 percent more efficient than elsewhere, producing a higher type of employee."

One group of employees, however, seems never to have been able to find ideal working conditions in the West, and that extended to the Napa Valley. As an 1852 account stated: "In short, there is a strong feeling—prejudice it may be—existing in California against all Chinamen, and they are nicknamed, cuffed about and treated very unceremoniously by every other class."

Chinese immigration intensified during the Gold Rush. In China stories were told of a place called California where gold was lying on the ground waiting to be picked up. It was a place where every man could become rich beyond his wildest dreams. Thousands of Chinese eagerly boarded ships in Canton or Shanghai expecting to find instant wealth when they landed in San Francisco. Unfortunately, upon arrival they found that the stories of the precious metal lying around everywhere were greatly exaggerated and that they needed equipment and supplies to search for the fabled gold. With few or no financial resources, most of these new immigrants were forced to work to pay for basic necessities and to try to make preparations to head for the mines. At this time the Chinese recognized that the other men of San Francisco had two basic needs that they could supply—food and clean clothing. So they posted signs on their shacks, and Chinese restaurants and laundries were established.

Unfortunately the niche the Chinese immigrants seemed destined to fill in many areas was that of a cheap, expendable labor force. In the Napa Valley the Chinese found work picking grapes and hops in the early 1870s and by the late 1880s made up more than eighty-five percent of all the valley's agricultural laborers. Large numbers of Chinese workers performed the dangerous and dirty work of extracting cinnabar from Napa's mountains, and as late as 1901, the Oat Hill Mine still employed 150 Chinese as miners. Judging from contemporary accounts, it was the expendability of the Chinese as much as their value as workers that the mine operators sought. The Chinese "heathens" set dynamite charges, cleared rubble from blown shafts, guided ore carts, and occasionally were killed or maimed during these efforts.

Chinese men were also employed in the digging and excavating of several wine-aging cellars, notably those at Schramsburg and Beringer, which are still seen as engineering feats. Chinese stonemasons built many of the buildings and bridges that remain as landmarks to-

St. Helena's Chinatown was located south of Sulpher Creek. Photographed around 1890, it burned to the ground in 1908. Courtesy, Napa County Historical Society

day, and Chinese immigrants were also employed at the glove factory in St. Helena and at the tanneries in Napa. There was, however, vocal opposition expressed to the Chinese learning a trade, born of the fear that they would eventually take over "white men's jobs." Domestic service was one field in which they seemed to have had little white competition. Many of the Napa Valley's prominent and successful families of the late 1800s had one or more Chinese domestics in their households.

Napa, Calistoga, St. Helena, and Rutherford all had Chinatowns, and their populations ranged from 30 to 600 each. These towns were located on the outskirts of the city and seemed to bear the brunt of scorn, anger, and derision, written and oral, from their white neighbors. They were made up of closely situated wooden structures that usually included Chinese stores,

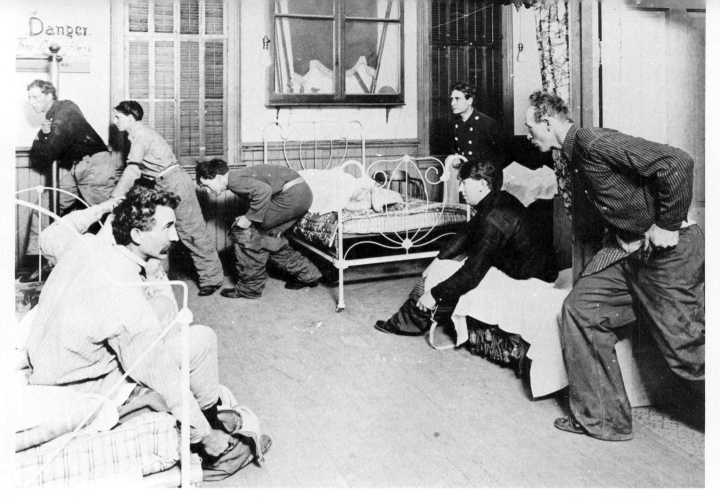

Above: *These gallant firemen of the Napa City Firehouse, on Second Street between Randolph and Coombs, were answering an early twentieth century call. Courtesy, Napa County Historical Society*

Right: *"Firebelle Lillie" Hitchcock Coit appears refined and sedate in this 1862 portrait. Lillie, who as a young woman resided in the valley on her parent's estate, acquired her nickname by her involvement with the firefighters of San Francisco's Knickerbocker Number Five Company. Rescued from a fire by them when she was a child, she was made an honorary member of the company. At her death, she left money to build a monument in San Francisco to her firemen—Coit Tower. Courtesy, California State Library*

wash houses or laundries, a joss house or place of worship, and gambling and opium dens.

The Chinese attempted to continue their culture rather than adapt to American ways. While this caused numerous problems for them, it was seldom done out of a sense of superiority. Almost all of the Chinese immigrants saw themselves as visitors. They had come with the intention of making enough money to support the family they had left behind in China. Most sent their earnings home, which upset Anglo neighbors who would rather have seen the money stay in the community. The Chinese attempted to keep their religious and social structure intact for the day they would return to China. In fact, if a Chinese man died in America, his body was shipped back to China, unless he was extremely poor or had no family to pay for it. The Chinese believed they had to return to join their ancestors.

While anti-Chinese feelings in the valley don't appear to have been extraordinary (many other communities had Anti-Chinese Leagues similar to those found in the valley), there does not seem to have been unusually strong benevolence either. Finally, after Congress passed the Chinese Exclusion Act in 1882 forbidding the further immigration of Chinese and denying U.S. citizenship to Chinese born in China, the tide seemed to turn. The number of new Chinese workers in the valley declined, and after having their towns burn several times and other incidents occur which implied they were unwelcomed, most Chinese were convinced to move away. Several families managed to stay on in the valley, though, and many years later, when attitudes finally allowed positive Chinese-American relations, Chinese contributions to the valley could be recognized for their value. Although virtually all remnants of Chinese settlement are gone, stories of their tenacity and industriousness have left an indelible mark on the spirit of the valley.

In much the same way that the valley is richer for its Chinese experience, it was also blessed by having experienced the incredible personality of Samuel Brannan. Sam Brannan was born in Saco, Maine, in 1819. As a young man, he had moved south, settling in New York and working as a printer for Joseph Smith and his Mormons and as a traveling companion for Smith's evangelizing brother. Historians are divided on Brannan's motives concerning his involvement with the Mormon Church. He is seen either as a leader and perhaps the right-

Right: *Sam Brannan spent $500,000 to develop his elaborate Calistoga resort in the valley's Hot Springs Township. The completed resort opened in 1862. Due to business reverses and a hefty divorce settlement, however, Brannan had to sell most of the resort in 1875. Fourteen years later he died a penniless man. Courtesy, California Historical Society. From Cirker,* Dictionary of American Portraits, *Dover, 1967*

ful heir to Joseph Smith's position, or as a scoundrel with a larcenous heart who used the Church and its tithes for his private gain. It is agreed, however, that in 1846 Brannan led the party of New York Mormons who left by ship for the West and the New Zion or Promised Land. He saw to their safe arrival in San Francisco and settled them there and in a colony he established on the Stanislaus River. He did collect tithes, which by various accounts were used either to establish the Mormons or himself in

Top: *Not only was this photo taken by the noted photographer Eadweard Muybridge at Napa County's Calistoga Springs resort, but also the subjects themselves are notable. The wagon holds California General Mariano Vallejo and several of his daughters. Vallejo is driving the wagon. Courtesy, California State Library*

Above and Facing Page, top: *Eadweard Muybridge took these photos at the Calistoga Springs resort in Napa County. The photos shown are actually half of a stereo photo. When the double stereo images were put in a stereoscope, a three-dimensional photo was seen. Courtesy, California State Library*

the new land. Brannan did walk from San Francisco to Utah to tell Brigham Young of the Zion he had found on the West Coast, but he was denied by Young who felt he, himself, had found the Promised Land of the Mormons on the shores of the Great Salt Lake.

After Brannan returned to San Francisco, he seems to have changed. Whether Sam saw Young's decision not to travel farther west as evidence that he would never be a leader of his Church and that his Zion would go unrecognized, or whether he felt relieved of close scrutiny by Young, Brannan took the opportunity to establish himself as a power in the community and begin to amass a personal fortune.

Brannan started the second newspaper in California and began buying businesses and real estate in both San Francisco and Sutterville (Sacramento). In 1848 it was Sam Brannan who announced to the world that gold had been discovered in California. His mercantile interests in San Francisco and Sutterville proved to be gold mines in themselves, and by 1856 Sam Brannan was considered the richest and best-known citizen of the new state.

Although White Sulpher Springs had been established as the valley's first resort in 1855, Sam Brannan's purchase in 1859 of 2,000 acres upvalley, including hot springs, signalled the real beginnings of the flamboyant resort era in the Napa Valley. Brannan had been impressed by the health resorts he visited in upper New York State while travelling with the Smiths, and had been further influenced by the claims of European health spas. He was now determined to build his own resort in the Napa Valley that would rival all others. At the time that Brannan arrived upvalley, Hot Springs Township was a small, quiet community. Sam Brannan would soon change that.

After spending about $500,000, Brannan

had a resort of which he could be justifiably proud. Centered around an elaborate Victorian hotel were bathhouses, twenty-five individual cottages along two avenues, a skating rink, dance pavillion, and an observatory and reservoir atop Mount Lincoln, which he had renamed for the new President. Adjoining all that were forty acres of stables and race track, home to Brannan's blooded horses which at one time numbered almost 1,000. Nearby were Brannan's agricultural endeavors, including a tea plantation, a grove of mulberry trees to house his silkworms, and grapevines which would supply his brandy distillery. He also imported 500 Merino sheep, but because he refused to build fences, his expensive sheep were thought to have been disposed of by angry neighbors tired of having their crops ruined.

Brannan did have a sense for extravagance. To celebrate the opening of his resort, he chartered a ship to bring a few thousand guests from San Francisco to Napa. He then had his guests transported by stage and carriage up the valley to his resort, where the celebration continued with generous supplies of food and drink. It has become somewhat of a legend that at this event Hot Springs Township was rechristened Calistoga by none other than Sam Brannan himself. He had apparently been imbibing quite liberally and when he rose to make the announcement that he had created a resort to rival those in the East, truly the "Saratoga of California" his words were slurred into the "Calistoga of Sarafornia." The name stuck. Although this account has yet to be adequately substantiated, it does serve as a reminder of the interest, excitement, and vitality that Brannan brought to the upper Napa Valley.

Soon after the resort opening, Sam Brannan embarked on his next major project: a railroad line to bring his guests, and others, up the val-

Above: *When Brannan's resort was finally sold piecemeal, all that remained were a few cottages and the palms. This circa 1900 view of the remains of the Calistoga resort looks northeast from the Calistoga Hotel. It was realized too late that Brannan had, "done more, perhaps, than any one or two other men for Napa County." Photo by Turrill and Miller. Courtesy, The Society of California Pioneers*

Napa Soda Springs Resort, with its magnificent rotunda and adjacent outbuildings and baths, was truly a marvelous creation. With views of Mt. Tamalpais in Marin County, Mt. Diablo in Contra Costa County, and the Napa Valley itself, it occupied an idyllic location. The resort was destroyed by fire in March of 1944. Courtesy, Napa County Historical Society

ley from the ferry landing at Suscol to Calistoga. Never being one to do things subtly or simply, Brannan created a furor in the valley over public funding of the line that eventually ended up being decided in the California State Legislature. But Sam Brannan got his railroad.

The first railroad in Napa County operated from Soscol Wharf to the down section of Napa City. Construction was begun in 1864 and completed in July of 1865. It was later extended to Calistoga, and that section was completed in 1868. The railroad seemed at its opening to be the answer to the valley's transportation needs. To celebrate its completion, Brannan threw another party, one for 3,000. The guest list included most of the notables of the day. James Lick, Mark Hopkins, Leland Stanford, and Collis P. Huntington all graced Sam's resort with their presence.

Unfortunately for Sam Brannan, and perhaps for the Napa Valley, both the railroad and Brannan's resort were doomed to fail. By 1869 the railroad was sold to the California Pacific Railroad Company. The Napa line had not generated enough revenue to meet expenses and Brannan was no longer able to keep it afloat personally. Shortly after this, because of some business reverses and a divorce settlement requiring Brannan to furnish his ex-wife with half of his assets in cash, Sam Brannan was forced to give up his Calistoga. The bank holding the mortgage on the resort ordered its sale and, except for the main building and a few cottages, Brannan's Hot Springs Resort was sold off in twenty-five to two hundred-acre parcels. Leland Stanford owned the main resort until 1919, having, at one point, considered locating his college there. Remnants of the resort may be seen now as Pacheteau's Original Hot Springs, and one of the cottages is preserved as an Historic Landmark adjoining the Sharpsteen Museum on Washington Avenue.

Sam Brannan never recovered from his financial reverses, even though he attempted several other schemes, including development of a colony in Mexico. He is said to have died quietly, broke and, perhaps, alone in Escondido. But he left a legacy behind in the upper Napa Valley. Calistoga is all the richer for having been Brannan's stepchild.

Though the Brannan Hot Springs Resort may appear extravagant in the extreme now, a hundred years ago, life, especially for the well-to-do, was quite different. During the late nineteenth and early twentieth centuries, San Francisco was a business and financial center and home to many prominent and successful families. Leisure time, especially for his wife and children, was a sign of a man's achievement. It was customary for a man of the house to deposit his family in a safe, secure, and socially acceptable resort for months at a time, visiting them on weekends. Since modern transportation systems were still some years in the future, holiday resorts had to be fairly close to home to avoid unnecessary time delays and the trauma associated with long-distance travel. The Napa Valley proved an ideal getaway location for San Franciscans. Not only did the valley boast an ideal climate (especially attractive to fog-bound San Franciscans) and beautiful landscapes, but it was also a short eighty miles away by ferry.

In addition the valley had health-giving spring waters in abundance. In the late 1800s the mineral springs at Napa Soda Springs were described as "among the most noted in the state." Carbonated spring water was first bottled here and was "highly esteemed as a beverage" and "an efficient aid to digestion, being antacid and tonic." In 1924 Guiseppe Musante first produced Hot Sulpher Geyser Water in Calistoga and for many years his company bottled water for the Calistoga Sparkling Mineral Water label. During the 1970s, with the new demand for sparkling water, the Calistoga Mineral Water Company resumed bottling and was purchased by Perrier in 1981. Other Napa Valley spring water companies include the Crystal Geyser Water Company, A. 'Sante Water Company, and the Napa Valley Springs Mineral Water Company.

In addition to its bottled waters, Napa Soda Springs provided resort accommodations equal to any prominent family's needs. In the manner of the late nineteenth century, the central building or rotunda was a landmark in itself. It was a seventy-five-foot-high circular building with a huge glass cupola on top. Its grand central parlor was 100 feet in diameter and was lighted by a forty-light gas chandelier. Sur-

The Petrified Forest was another early tourist attraction bringing visitors upvalley to gaze at the rocks that had once been giant trees. Found and developed by Charles Evans, "Petrified Charlie," it too continues as an attraction. Photo by Turrill and Miller. Courtesy, Napa County Historical Society

rounding the rotunda, on different elevations, were the guest accommodations, all with gas and running water. There was a clubhouse with billiard and bagatelle tables, bowling alleys, and lawn tennis and croquet grounds. The resort covered over 1,000 acres and also provided guests with bathing facilities with both hot and cold spring water. The swimming bath alone measured one hundred and fifty feet in length and fifty feet in width and varied in depth from four to ten feet.

Here at Napa Soda Springs or at neighboring White Sulphur Springs or Aetna Springs resorts, a successful San Francisco family could rent, lease, or even purchase accommodations. They could hobnob with others of their social station. The women would have amiable company during their extended stays and their children could meet acceptable young ladies or gentlemen.

With the advent of automobile and, later, airplane transportation, came the beginning of the end of the early resort era in the Napa Valley. By World War II, most of the nineteenth-century resorts had declined into oblivion as more people could afford to spend their vacations in faraway, exotic lands. Later, due to neglect, fire, and vandalism, most of the valley's resorts ceased to exist.

The Excelsior Brass Band, pictured here about 1913, provided Napa residents with a respite from their labors in the early twentieth century. It was the successor to the Juarez Napa Band. Courtesy, Napa County Historical Society

Chapter 6

CHANGING VISTAS

While some were enjoying the carefree and sheltered world of the valley's resorts, war broke out in Europe. With the outbreak of World War I in August 1914, previously unknown European place-names such as Somme, Verdun, and Aisne became headline news throughout the country, and Napa County was no exception. Virtually every offensive in Europe was documented as the relentless battles between the Allied and Axis armies took place. Though the United States had not yet entered the war, day after day the clash remained a major topic of discussion due to the valley's relatively large population of those of Italian and German ancestry. The "war to end all wars" took on a much more personal note, however, with America's entry into the conflict.

Ten million men registered for "war service" in 1917, of which 687,000 were needed in the first call for the national army. A random lottery was conducted to choose those to be drafted for war. Quotas were established for each local draft board, which had the responsibility to induct those registered according to their lottery position. Napa County's first quota was 134 men.

All of Napa County waited with anticipation at 9:30 a.m. on July 20, 1917, when the first Napans' serial numbers were selected in the "great national lottery" held in a committee room of the Senate office building in Washington, D.C.

As the number 258, that of Bruce Land of Napa, became the first to be drawn for Napa County, the once remote European place-names suddenly became household words. Throngs of people surrounded the courthouse in Napa where the list of those drafted was posted.

The first detachment of Napa County's young soldiers was ordered to leave Napa on September 8. Their destination was the WWI training camp at American Lake, Washington. District Attorney Frank Coombs, acting on behalf of the County, requested that all businesses close so that as many citizens as possible could bid the men farewell. With the Napa Band as an escort, the soldiers marched from the Armory to the Southern Pacific Depot.

As the weeks and months went by, the march to the depot became an all too frequent scene. The newspaper and printing businesses became drawn even closer to the war when the *Napa Register* lost one of its employees to the draft, and Raymond Prouty, the linotype operator for the *St. Helena Photogram* and son of the editor, Harry Prouty, was inducted. The sentiments of the *Register* were sincere when it stated that, "As the weeks go by and the young

men of Napa County selected for military service march away to the training camps the grim reality of war is drawn closer and closer home to the people of this community. . . . the heartstrings are tense and emotions arise which surely try those who are left behind."

The federal government had begun the sale of Liberty Bonds to aid in financing the war effort. In mid-1918 a Liberty Loan demonstration was held in Napa's Court House square. An enormous throng turned out to listen to the exercises and speeches, the Mare Island Training Camp Band, and to greet the 300 sailors from Mare Island that came for the extravaganza. The Boy Scouts from Napa who had sold the greatest number of bonds were presented with medals by Napa Judge Henry Gesford, and a fiery anti-German, anti-pacifist, and anti-IWW (the International Workers of the World) speech was given by Judge C.E. McLaughlin of Sacramento. The large crowd punctuated his inspirational speech with cheers and were very much in support of what McLaughlin said. Napa County's sentiments were definitely patriotic.

Toward the latter part of 1918, however, the

war was beginning to take its toll on the spirits of the community. While still fiercely patriotic and still supportive of the American effort in the war, a weariness could be detected among the valley's citizenry as the draft marches wore on. A change in tone occurred even in the printed news about the draft lottery. Instead of reflecting the sentiments of those left behind, the *Napa Daily Journal* of October 1918 stated unemotionally, if not somewhat cynically, that President Wilson was again to draw the first names from the "big glass bowl holding the fate of the nation's 18-45 [year old] human war material."

Fortunately, it was only a matter of weeks before the war ended and an armistice was signed. Upon news of the end of the fighting, the mayor of Napa granted a half-day holiday. All stores and saloons closed as throngs of people rushed into the streets to celebrate. A parade was held with the drum and bugle corps, city officials, the fire department, and the Red Cross, to name a few, participating. The festivities continued far into the night as bells rang, bands played, sirens shrieked, and firecrackers exploded.

Perhaps the most joyful group were the sixty-three men who were to be inducted into the United States Army at the courthouse that day, but who had their orders cancelled due to the armistice. The marches from the Armory to the depot had ended.

Throughout the 1920s, Napa County politically mirrored the rest of the country. From 1920 to 1930, the county had voted Republican in each gubernatorial election, and no Democratic partisan candidate won an election in the county. However, as was documented in an earlier chapter, the impact of Prohibition had exacted a great toll on the wineries and their labor force in the Napa Valley. This af-

Above: *Napa's draftees were taken to Fort Lewis, Washington, a major World War I training camp. Shown here are Andy Freeze from Oroville and Louis Guisto and Walter Poncietta of Napa (top row). Also shown are Jack Leffingwell, John Jackson, and Leonard Roberts of Napa (bottom row). Guisto, who had played professional baseball for Philadelphia before the war, had to resign his position after being gassed in France. Courtesy, Napa County Historical Society*

Facing page: *During World War I inductees gathered in front of Napa's courthouse to hear Judge Gesford deliver a farewell address to them. Shown here is the contingent of young men selected for military service on October 8, 1917. After being presented with silk flags (note two flags in front row), the group marched to the depot to board the train for Fort Lewis. Courtesy, Napa County Historical Society*

fected the county's voting habits.

While the Great Depression had not yet hit California as hard as the other regions of the country, its effects were significant enough to cause Californians, including those of Napa County, to vote Democratic in the 1932 Presidential election. However, Napa County still voted for A.L. Tubbs, a Republican candidate for the Senate, in the 1932 direct primary election. Tubbs only took a handful of California's counties, but Napa was one of them. A "wet" Republican, Tubbs opposed Prohibition in the field of "wet" vs. "dry" candidates. The county had voted for Franklin Delano Roosevelt, but otherwise remained strongly Republican.

While the Great Depression affected all of the United States, Napa County fared little worse than the rest of California. Due to its rural, agricultural nature and relatively small population, the impact of the Depression on the valley was relatively mild. With the repeal of Prohibition in 1933, grapes and wine were again in demand. But the impact, even though lessened, was still there.

A comparative look at the economic effect of World War I, the Depression, and World War II on the faculty of the private Pacific Union College (PUC) in the Napa Valley community of Angwin illustrates the point. During World War I the faculty of PUC received yearly cost of living bonuses and were relatively well-off. These bonuses ceased with the end of the war, but salaries nevertheless continued to climb to as high as forty dollars a week by 1926. The Depression produced paycuts and staff reductions, and one-teacher departments were created whenever possible. In 1933, as an austerity measure, the college science department even recommended "do-it-yourself procurement of laboratory cats." By 1934 the top salary was only thirty dollars per week. Recovery was slow, and it was not until 1941 and the advent of World War II that the 1926 level was again reached.

The Napa Valley was also the recipient of many of the beneficial effects of F.D.R.'s recovery program. The 1933 National Industrial Recovery Act included formation of the Public Works Administration (PWA). A major project of the PWA in the valley was the improvement of the Silverado Trail in 1936. Trees were cleared, brush removed, and portions of the trail near Glass Mountain were blasted, as part of the road's improvement. Dams were also constructed and the valley's waterworks improved. The PWA planned these major, long-term projects then contracted with local firms for the construction itself.

The Civilian Conservation Corps had a

Top: *Civic organizations have filled an important niche throughout Napa County's history. From early agricultural associations to modern business groups, civic organizations such as the Napa Lions Club have contributed to the improvement of the quality of life in the valley. This photo dates from about 1940. Courtesy, Napa County Historical Society*

camp at the upper end of Napa County which provided work for the unemployed.

The Works Progress Administration (WPA) developed a program that was designed to help white-collar workers and artists as well as laborers. The WPA instituted Federal Project Number 1, which established projects in art, music, theater, and writing. One of these, the Historical Records Survey, developed an inventory of Napa County's archival resources. They located documents, organized them, developed an index and bibliography, all of which remain an invaluable resource today.

Above: *As the automobile grew in popularity as a form of transportation, major construction projects took place to accommodate them. Roads were widened and paved, and new concrete bridges, such as Napa's Third Street bridge, replaced earlier wooden structures. Courtesy, Napa County Historical Society*

Another segment of the WPA was the Federal Writer's Project. One of its efforts was the publication of *California: A Guide to the Golden State,* which included the Napa Valley.

While these federal projects provided the Napa Valley with needed assistance, it was the increased activity generated by the demands of World War II that restored the economic base of the county. By the end of 1941, building activity in Napa County had set an all-time record. Retail sales soared. One of the major reasons for this economic spurt was the proximity of Vallejo's Mare Island Naval Shipyard, which constructed naval vessels. One-fifth of the more than 25,000 workers at the Navy's shipbuilding facility lived in Napa County. All required housing and services. The commute problem this created between Napa and Vallejo necessitated major highway construction programs. Upgrading the Napa-Vallejo highway was required since it was part of the national defense highway system. By the end of 1941 Napa County's unemployment insurance payments amounted to $3,141 as compared to $13,764 one year earlier.

In 1942 the Basalt Rock Company of Napa launched two U.S. navy tankers on the Napa River. The U.S.S. *Crownblock* and the U.S.S. *Whipstock* were the first major ships constructed in Napa County.

Due to the proximity of the war construction effort to the city of Napa, air raid rules and blackout and defense procedures were developed. The city council even adopted an ordinance that allowed peace officers, during a blackout, to enter any building in which a light was visible and extinguish it, using "reasonable force" if necessary.

The war took on a new reality for county residents when nineteen-year-old David Lyttle became the valley's first casualty. Lyttle died in

action in Manila.

World War II presented dual ironies to Napa. On the one hand, Napa's population boomed. It gained 13,500 residents between 1940 and 1943, a population increase of over 30 percent. But farmers had ever-increasing problems getting field help for their harvests due to the attractive wages in war industries and because of the selective service draft. Although the losses were not devastating, the county's tomato and prune harvest could not be completed one year.

While housing construction increased and retailers prospered on the one hand, gasoline and tires were rationed and farm machinery became almost non-existent on the other. An economic shift from agriculture to industry had occurred. However, the change would not be permanent since the industrial complexes were on the periphery of Napa, and not in the agricultural heartland. When World War II ended, the valley's economy quickly reverted back to its agricultural base. Major industries, such as the Basalt Rock Co., which continued to prosper after the war, were located downvalley. Napa had remained a bedroom community for the war industry, which left its scenic qualities and its fertile future intact.

Described as a modern Eden by some, blessed with idyllic weather, incredible scenic beauty, close (but not too close) proximity to urban areas, and a stable economy, the valley moved into the second half of the twentieth century with indicators pointing toward success and contentment. But every silver lining seems to have a cloud and storms appear to be brewing to threaten even this clime.

Water and the supply or lack of it may eventually be seen as the major issue facing the Napa Valley. The availability of water in the Napa Valley was one of the major determinants

in the early settlement of the area. Unfortunately for those settlers, the Napa River was prone to flooding in heavy rainfall years and it did not produce enough runoff for the area's population during years of low precipitation.

Opposite, top: *A circa 1940 photo of downtown Napa shows the automobile as part of the urban scene. Courtesy, Napa County Historical Society*

Above: *The narrow Napa Valley has been susceptible to periodic flooding during periods of unusually heavy rainfall. In 1940 the Napa River reached flood stage. Courtesy, Napa County Historical Society*

By 1922 the water supply for the city of Napa had become inadequate. That year the city purchased the privately held Napa City Water Company and formed a municipal system. In 1923 construction began on a dam on Millikan Creek to augment the inadequate system. Completed in 1924, Millikan Dam still supplies the city's water system.

The 1940s saw a boom in construction as World War II created jobs for thousands of workers in Vallejo's shipyards, making Napa a residential area for those defense employees. Conn Dam was also constructed to increase the water supply to Napa's still-growing population. It was completed in 1948.

During the next decade the city of Napa continued its growth pattern and its need for water increased. The beautiful Berryessa Valley, which was the largest wheat-producing area of the county, was dammed and flooded to help supply Napa's thirsty population. The dam and reservoir at Berryessa were part of the California Water Project, the goal of which was to meet the flood-control needs of Northern California and the urban water demands of Southern California. In accomplishing this mission, Napa County lost its Berryessa Valley and gained a large, recreational lake.

In 1976 and 1977 a severe drought struck California. In the Napa Valley many of the vineyards, as well as the city of Calistoga, experienced a water shortage of crisis proportions. Wells were drilled deeper to supply the arid vineyards, while a building moratorium and water rationing were placed on Calistoga's populace.

When the drought ended in 1978, provisions were made to eventually complete a water supply pipeline to the upper Napa Valley. Although rationing continued intermittently in Calistoga, the new system should insure that water

Between the night of February 13, 1986, and the morning of February 17, fourteen to twenty inches of almost nonstop rain inundated all Napa County communities. Then, shortly after 7:00 a.m. on February 17, the Napa River overflowed its banks, causing what residents referred to as the "Flood of the Century." The photos reproduced on these pages and the following page show only some of the damage and dislocation caused by the deluge. All photos appear courtesy of the Napa Register.

shortages will not occur again to create the nightmares it did in that little city. It was an ironic twist that Calistoga's famous bottled water was increasing rapidly in popularity and production during the same period that Calistoga's municipal water system was failing.

Depending on key decisions made concerning the water supply, other potential problems may appear. Since the valley is seen as a positive environment for living, the pressure to house the Bay Area's workers may well increase. If sufficient water ceases to be a concern, then valley residents will be faced with the issue of growth control for the sake of preserving the valley's identity.

Deciding who or how many may live in an area has always been a difficult, thankless task and it promises to be all the more difficult when the issue of preserving agricultural lands is added. In 1968 the Napa County Board of Supervisors, acting to protect the prime land on the valley floor, limited subdivision of that preserve land to twenty acres or more. In addition to creating this agricultural preserve, it established tax protection for its farmers. But the pressure of development may one day threaten even this designation.

In addition to permanent population increases, the valley has to deal with increases in visitor population. In 1968 the Christian Brothers Greystone Winery, for example, had 150,000 visitors. During 1983, 400,000 visitors toured and tasted at that facility. Since both transportation arteries serving the valley are, for the most part, two-lane roads, traffic congestion has become a problem. For cities like St. Helena and Calistoga, whose main street is also Highway 29, this additional traffic causes more than a little aggravation. Some wonder if the ambiance of the valley can be preserved if new, wider highways are constructed to handle the increased load.

With escalating auto traffic has come a renewed concern about air quality in the valley. Grapes are a very sensitive crop. The chemicals which create air pollution such as that generated in the Bay Area are detrimental to the quality of the grapes which are effected. So pollution is a real threat to the continued excellence of wine produced in the Napa Valley.

Added to pollutants from increasing auto exhaust and from Bay Area industries which may drift or be blown into the valley, is the potential for the fouling of the air by geothermal drilling. The Calistoga area is still active geothermally, and proposals to produce energy as well as minerals by extracting the steam being held underground seem to surface more than occasionally. Another oil or energy crisis may necessitate the production of geothermal energy and force the valley to deal with its inherent side effects.

While it may appear that the burden of preserving and protecting the valley while assuring the good life for its citizens will be a monumental task, valley residents, like their forebearers, seem to be up to the challenge. Perhaps one of the reasons for this is that people in the valley have chosen not to forget earlier times and people. The Napa County Historical Society, which has been the force in the valley for decades, preserves not only the Goodman Library as its headquarters, but is also an outstanding repository for photographs and documents, some dating back to the Spanish period. In Calistoga an extremely talented and energetic man, Ben Sharpsteen, spent his retirement years establishing a museum to preserve the history of Calistoga and its famous citizen, Sam Brannan. Mr. Sharpsteen, an Academy Award-winning Walt Disney artist and producer, sought to develop a sense of pride in and understanding of Calistoga while preserving reminders of its special character. The Sharpsteen Museum stands as a monument both to the city's builder, Sam Brannan, and to the man who helped preserve its history, Ben Sharpsteen.

Downvalley in St. Helena there are two special repositories located in the St. Helena Library. One is the Wine Library, which is a valuable collection of information both on wines and wine making and on the Napa Valley. The Robert Louis Stevenson Museum is also located in the library building. The Vailima Foundation has assembled an unmatched collection of Stevenson memorabilia and manuscripts there. Although Stevenson only spent a short time in the Napa Valley, it affected him deeply and his effect on the valley is shown here at the museum established in his honor.

Between Calistoga and St. Helena stands another monument to the valley's past and its ingenuity. The grist mill of Dr. Edward Turner Bale, built around 1846, had the largest overshot waterwheel west of the Mississippi. Its size was directly related to summer shortages of water in the valley creating the need for the most efficient mill-drive system that could be implemented. The wheel was eventually replaced, first by a steam engine and then by a water turbine. As crops changed, the need for the mill declined until it was shut down in 1905. In 1923 the widow of the mill's last owner, W.W. Lyman, Sr., deeded the mill to the Native Sons of the Golden West for preservation as a public monument. Due to the high cost of maintenance, the Native Sons turned it over to Napa County in 1941 to continue preservation efforts. In 1974 the mill was transferred to the State of California and became Bale Grist Mill State Historic Park. Using money from the 1980 Park Bond Act, the California Depart-

ment of Parks and Recreation painstakingly restored the mill structure. With the financial assistance of the California State Parks Foundation, the mill equipment will be restored and, hopefully, the mill wheel will turn again.

Coupled with a remembrance of their past, Napa Valley people also seem to have retained their predecessors' willingness to change and adapt without losing their sense of purpose. From the very obvious decision of the Tuckers not to follow the path chosen by the Donner Party to the resourcefulness of Josephine Tychson, who took over the family winery after her husband's death in the 1880s and became one of the first female vintners in America, adversity has seemed to bring out the best in Napa Valley's people. Their willingness to change has allowed them and their valley to persevere.

While change has been seen as a solution, it has also been sought as an improvement. The innovative wine-making techniques coming out of the valley are changing the industry. Cooperative ventures with European wine makers promise more excitement and innovation, and quite probably even better wines. From the women of the nineteenth-century Callustro Company, who produced a cleaning product they felt was superior and had the panache to market it worldwide, to the current international implications of wine and mineral water production, the valley has seldom been shy about promoting its products. And it has, for the most part, had the very finest quality products to promote.

It is small wonder then that the Napa Valley holds such an attraction. From the earlier time of golden fields to the modern era of purple harvest, it has been a special place with special products and very special people. To experience the Napa Valley is truly to know paradise.

Grapevines creep over the rolling hills of Calistoga, enhancing the beauty of the valley. Photo by Mark E. Gibson

Left: *The purple bounty of the Inglenook vineyards grows in the town of Rutherford. Photo by C.W. May/Terraphotographics/ BPS*

Facing page: *The rich rust and verdant vegetation of the valley as captured in the photo at top is almost duplicated in Sara Barnes' acrylic painting at bottom titled* Towards Diamond Mountain. *Photo by Mark E. Gibson. Painting courtesy of Barbara W. Ryan, The Gallery on Main Street, St. Helena, California*

The Napa Valley landscape bursts with color in the fall. Photo by John Elk III

Facing page and top: *Early morning low clouds and mist hang over the valley, bestowing an ethereal quality on the area and providing an ideal setting for photographer and painter alike. Photos by John Elk III. Watercolor painting,* Morning Mist, *by Dave Huddleston. Painting courtesy of Barbara W. Ryan, The Gallery on Main Street, St. Helena, California*

Above: *Depicted in watercolors by Dave Huddleston is St. Helena's Ehlers Lane. Courtesy, Barbara W. Ryan, The Gallery on Main Street, St. Helena, California*

The valley is home to a number of nineteenth-century structures. The Richie Block in St. Helena dates from 1892. Photo by John Elk III

Gustave Niebaum, like other nineteenth-century vintners in the valley, spared no expense in constructing a solidly built, yet aesthetically pleasing, winery and cellar. Photo by John Elk III

Soaring silently over the valley in a glider is a unique experience not to be missed. During the 1950s and 1960s soaring became popular as a sport, and in 1968 the Calistoga Soaring Center opened. Photo by Mark E. Gibson

Since the early 1900s the "Old Faithful" geyser has attracted visitors to the upper Napa Valley. The geyser shoots a stream of steam and hot water about 100 feet into the air. Photo by K.E. Lindquist/Terraphotographics/BPS

Hot-air ballooning has really taken off as a popular activity for tourists and residents to partake in. From a balloon, one sees a spectacular view of the valley. Photo by John Elk III

Chapter 7

PARTNERS IN PROGRESS

George Calvert Yount, the first white settler to come to the Napa Valley, made his way by horseback to the top of Mt. St. Helena. Standing atop that mountain, observing the panoramic view of the entire Napa Valley, he stated: "In such a place I would like to clear the land and make my home, in such a place I would like to live and die."

It seems that many of the people who have settled in the Napa Valley shared his sentiment. This beautiful fertile valley enjoys a typical Mediterranean climate with mild, wet winters and warm, dry summers. The climate and the Napa River, coupled with the close proximity to San Francisco, have been instrumental in the development of the county.

As far back as the Indian era the river played an important role in the lives of area inhabitants. The Indians depended on the river for both food and transportation. Trout and salmon were plentiful. Unlike other Indians who traveled by horseback, the Napa County Indians traveled either on foot or by river raft.

In the early days people were transported in and out of Napa County by steamer, and commerce was centered around the river for easy shipping and receiving of goods. In addition, the climate proved conducive to the resort era. Wealthy San Franciscans came to the Napa Valley to escape the congestion of the city much as they do today.

The fertile soil of the region has attracted people interested in agriculture from all parts of the world. Agriculture and mining greatly influenced the commercial and industrial growth of Napa County. With the influx of immigrants, the lumber industry also developed. Wheat brought flour mills, viticulture brought wineries, and orchards brought dehydrators and packing plants to process fruits. Later Napa became known for the manufacture of men's and women's apparel, gloves, and shoes.

The Napa Valley was settled by hardy people who developed a deep sense of community. They came because they were willing to work hard to maintain the "good life." Though the way they do business has changed, the spirit of Napa Valley residents has not.

The organizations whose stories are detailed on the following pages have chosen to support this important literary and civic project. They illustrate the variety of ways in which individuals and their businesses have contributed to the area's growth and development. The civic involvement of the Napa Valley's business, institutions of learning, and local government, in cooperation with its citizens, has made the area an excellent place to live and work.

NAPA COUNTY HISTORICAL SOCIETY

The Napa County Historical Society is housed in the famous old Goodman Library building, the cornerstone for which was laid May 2, 1901. The picturesque native-stone structure was a gift to the city from George E. Goodman, a member of a prominent banking family of Napa. Today it is being used by the society as a research library and museum. This is the oldest library in California still being used for its original purpose.

Jess Doud—current executive director of the society—worked with the Goodman heirs, Napa City Council, and the City-County Library Commisson to finalize all the necessary details to secure a permanent home for the society. On July 21, 1975, an agreement was signed with the City of Napa whereby the society was granted occupancy of the Goodman Library for a period of fifty-five years. On April 4, 1976, the doors of the Goodman Library were once again opened to the community, and the society held a general membership meeting in the former children's story room on the first floor.

The group had come a long way from its first formation meeting held on April 16, 1948, in the Plaza Hotel in downtown Napa. May 8 was selected as the date for the first public meeting, because of its historical significance as the 100th anniversary of news of the Coloma Gold discovery being proclaimed in Napa City. The site of the meeting was the Old Bale Mill north of St. Helena, where a picnic was held for members and other interested persons. In 1970 the Old Bale Mill was adopted as the hallmark of the society, with the design being done by Mrs. Bernice T. Sharpsteen.

On May 14, 1948, the society became a nonprofit corporation under the laws of the State of California and remains so to this day. It was es-

tablished to study the history of the state, with emphasis on Napa County, and to collect and preserve the artifacts of the native and pioneer people. One recent project that Doud was instrumental in getting under way was to create community awareness that Napa was the "Birthplace of the Loudspeaker." On May 18, 1985, a bronze plaque was laid in front of the house at 1606 F Street, where Peter L. Jensen and Edwin S. Pridham first established their laboratory in March 1911. In May 1915 they developed the "dynamic loud-speaking telephone." Later the name was changed to "magnavox," meaning "great voice."

Additionally, the group produces three publications. In May 1970 *Gleanings,* a monogram published periodically, came into print. In June

1971 the present newsletter, *Tidings,* was inaugurated; and February 1979 marked the beginning of *Sketches,* a publication of manuscripts from the society's archives. The Napa County Historical Society's holdings have grown from an empty historical building and a few dozen books in 1975 to a bulging depository of historical material. The membership has grown as well, from about 25 initial members to the present membership of over 712.

The famous old Goodman Library building. The cornerstone was laid May 2, 1901. The facility was a gift to the city from George E. Goodman, a prominent banker. This old building is presently being used as a library and museum by the Napa County Historical Society. It is the oldest library in the state of California still being used for its original purpose.

114

SILVERADO COUNTRY CLUB AND RESORT

The beautiful resort and country club known today simply as Silverado was built by General John F. Miller and his wife in the early 1870s. Following the Civil War he returned to California, where he had lived briefly before the war, and became collector of the Port of San Francisco. Later he began searching for a permanent homesite removed from the commercial activity of "The City." As a young attorney General Miller had lived in Napa and served as treasurer of Napa County in the 1850s, so he turned his sights to the Napa Valley. He was familiar with Rancho Yajome—formerly owned by Salvador Vallejo, brother of General Vallejo. Upon viewing this beautiful parcel of land with its rolling hills, wide meadows, groves of trees watered by sparkling Millikin Creek, and framed by the beautiful Napa hills, he knew he had reached the end of his search.

The 1,200-acre Silverado property was purchased by General and Mrs. Miller in several parcels. Upon completion of the property transfers, General Miller named his new estate Le Vergne in memory of the battle of Le Vergne—in which he first heard the whistle of a bullet fired by an enemy of the flag of his country.

Construction of the great mansion nestled in an idyllic grove of trees began in the early 1870s. The Millers designed their residence and the surrounding landscape to incorporate adaptations of Italian and French architecture. Behind the mansion is an unusual and beautiful 250-foot-long stone wall. Still standing in a perfect state of preservation, this wall is a remarkable example of the masonry skill of the era. The stones were painstakingly gathered from Millikin Creek.

The mansion was built to house many distinguished guests, among whom were President Theodore Roosevelt and John J. Pershing.

Mrs. Richardson Clover, daughter

The Mansion Le Vergne as it appears today—as the Silverado Country Club.

of General Miller, sold the estate in 1932 to Mrs. Vesta Peak Maxwell. In 1953 Mrs. Maxwell sold Le Vergne to a group organized as the Silverado Land Company, at which time the great estate was officially named Silverado.

Pat Markovich, one of the new owners and a golf professional, converted the mansion to a clubhouse and built an eighteen-hole golf course—and the original Silverado Country Club came into being. In 1966 the clubhouse and the 1,200-acre property were purchased by Westgate Development Company and American Factors of Honolulu (now known as Amfac, Inc.). Since then it has almost continuously been expanded and improved upon. Presently owned by Robert Meyer, it is

one of the nation's finest resorts—containing such attractions as two eighteen-hole golf courses and eight swimming pools, as well as twenty tennis courts, an executive conference center, and gracious restaurants. All assure uncompromising luxury accommodations for distinguished guests and corporate heads desiring a place to meet away from the stress of the business world.

Today a full-service resort and one of the major employers in Napa County, Silverado is a $25-million operation with a payroll of $8 million per year. During the eight-month prime season, it employs over 600 persons, 80 percent of whom have more than three to five years' seniority. As a hotel it gives in excess of $800,000 in bed taxes to Napa County each year. As a private country club, it has a membership of 700.

Yesterday, Le Vergne—today, Silverado. Both spell elegance and luxury.

BARWICK-DUTTONS STATIONERY AND OFFICE PRODUCTS

Little did Robert Barwick of Barwick-Duttons realize when his father convinced him that there was a need for an office products store in Napa that one day he would own one of the largest office products stores in the Bay Area outside of San Francisco.

Henry E. Barwick with his wife, Lillian, and two sons, Robert and Edward, moved to Napa from San Francisco on September 30, 1936. Henry had been in retail all of his life with his career beginning in 1910 as a temporary window trimmer at Schwartz and Goodman, a ladies' wear store on Market Street opposite Powell in San Francisco. He advanced to store manager in 1920 and remained in that capacity until the store closed in 1928. Barwick then went into business for himself, until in 1932 the Depression forced him out. He then accepted a position as manager of a department store in San Francisco for three and a half years, and had been unhappy with that position.

He was prompted to meet Walter Bamburg by a mutual friend. Bamburg owned Bamburg's Chicago Emporium in Napa and was looking for a manager in order to allow him more free time. Upon their meeting,

Barwick was offered the position. He accepted and prepared to move his family to Napa. However, house hunting became so discouraging that the move almost didn't take place. A house was finally found with the help of Walter Bamburg, and on September 30, 1936, the family boarded the ferry in San Francisco and made the trip to Vallejo and on to Napa—quite a journey at that time. Lillian was unhappy for the first six months but soon made the adjustment, and the family became actively involved in the community.

Robert first became involved with the business community through his high school newspaper, which he served as business manager. Upon graduation he went to work for the *Napa Register,* becoming circulation manager. He then went to work at Basalt until the Japanese attack on

---

Barwick Business Machines won the trophy for selling the most Royal typewriters from August 1, 1956, to July 31, 1957. Left to right: Earl Howard, vice-president and service manager; J. Hult, regional sales manager, Royal Typewriter Company; Vic Baumheffner, president, Royal Typewriter Company; Robert Barwick, secretary/manager, Barwick Business Machines; and Henry Barwick, president, Barwick Business Machines.

Pearl Harbor. Robert joined the Merchant Marines and graduated from the U.S. Merchant Marine Academy on Long Island, New York, in December 1943. While he was at sea his father wrote and informed him of the opportunity to purchase Duttons' Variety Store, which was located at that time at 1035 Main all the way through to 1034 Brown. It housed a wide range of products from clothing to pots and pans. It was also the only toy store open year-round in Napa.

Robert and Henry jointly invested in the business. However, when Robert returned to Napa his father convinced him that Napa needed an office products and stationery store. After some consideration, Robert decided to join his father to help him build up the stationery store. Robert worked as outside salesman while his father managed the business. Calling on local firms, he would take orders for office products and go to the city to purchase the items ordered, one for the customer and one for the shelf, thus building the stationery store's inventory. The office products business grew and became Duttons' Napa Stationery Store. Then Robert Barwick opened a satellite concern on Pearl Street called Barwick Business Machines, which was the Napa-Solano distributor for Victor adding machines and Royal typewriters from 1952 to 1981. The firm had six service technicians and two outside office machine salesmen; and in 1953 Earl Howard was hired as vice-president/service manager.

In November 1958 Duttons' Napa Stationery Store and Barwick Business Machines combined operations and moved to a two-story, 12,000-square-foot building at 1025 Main and 1024 Brown. The company remained there until progressing urban development forced a relocation. The Barwicks found it difficult to find a suitable site locally, so they searched from Susanville to Chula Vista with-

The firm's second site, after Duttons' Napa Stationery Store and Barwick Business Machines combined operations.

out success. Finally, an agreement was reached between the owner of Self's Market and Robert Barwick and they acquired the firm's present building at 3230 Jefferson Street. After making the transition from downtown to North Napa it took a year and a half to bring the business back to the point of the pre-move volume. The company lost 1,000 square feet and today is still 450 square feet shy of the earlier downtown location. What had been a traumatic situation was overcome, and Barwick-Duttons was opened August 9, 1971.

Henry remained active in the firm until 1976. Both Robert and Edward credit their father with their business success. Barwick-Duttons continues as a family operation, with Robert's wife, the former Florence Born, and his mother, Lillian, playing active roles. Later, after being widowed, Henry married Martha Streblow James and she too was actively involved in the venture for a time. Presently Robert Barwick is president and his wife, Florence, is vice-president, secretary, and chairman of the board. They have three chil-

dren: Cindy, Rob, and Jill.

Robert and Florence have taken active roles in community organizations, with Robert also being involved in the National Office Products Association. Robert is past president of the Napa Rotary and past district governor of the northwestern district of Rotary International. Florence is past chairman of the Entre Nous Women's Club of Napa. Robert has been district governor for California in the National Office Products Association and has served on various manufacturers' advisory councils for dealers.

Henry had instilled in his family the importance of treating employees and customers fairly, and claimed that a business would treat you as well as you treated it. Barwick-Duttons has become successful by following these precepts. Currently employing twenty-eight people, the firm serves Vacaville to Benicia and Vallejo to Calistoga with two outside salespeople. One of them, Jan Carruth, has worked in outside furniture sales since 1972. Many opportunities to advance in the industry are granted to the employees, with the company sponsoring ongoing training programs such as seminars and trade shows. The general manager is sent to Holyoke, Massachusetts, for training programs and seminars on paper products. From there the trip extends to the national convention and office products show in Chicago put on by the National Office Products Association. For fifteen years the employees have been bused to San Francisco to visit the annual trade show.

The present location of Barwick-Duttons Stationery and Office Products store was occupied by the firm on August 9, 1971.

PACIFIC UNION COLLEGE

Ellen G. White, author and spiritual leader of the Seventh-day Adventist Church, was instrumental in the founding of Pacific Union College.

Elder S.N. Haskell, president of the Pacific Union Conference of Seventh-day Adventists at the time Pacific Union College was being organized.

William C. White, son of Ellen G. White and first school board president, headed the efforts to establish Pacific Union College.

Mrs. Ellen G. White, author and spiritual leader of the Seventh-day Adventist Church, wrote: "The necessity of establishing Christian schools is very great. Schools are needed where the word of God is made the basis of education. As an educating power, it is of more value than the writings of all philosophers of all ages. Education has to do with the whole being and the whole period of existence possible to man. It is the harmonious development of the physical, the mental, and the spiritual powers. It prepares the student for the joy of service in this world, and for the higher joy of wider service in the world to come."

At the tenth annual session of the California Conference of Seventh-day Adventists in 1881, twenty-two years after Merritt G. Kellogg left Michigan to begin pioneering the faith on the West Coast, the western membership was aware of the need to provide proper schooling for its young people. White and her son, William C., were in attendance at that camp meeting. Convinced that the denomination's progress was sufficient to justify the immediate establishment of a western school, Ellen White personally and urgently appealed for the support of local landowners. The conference voted $2,000 for initial expenses. On October 20, 1881, a school board was organized with William White as president.

William White returned to Michigan in hopes of engaging Sidney Brownsberger as principal of the western school. For seven years Brownsberger had served as president of Battle Creek College. He agreed to come to California to help establish the school.

After some searching the Healdsburg Institute, built in 1877, became available. It was within the organization's price range, and on April 5, 1882, William White, acting for the board, purchased the facility for $3,750 in gold coin.

The Brownsbergers arrived in Oakland early in March 1882, and on April 11 the Healdsburg Academy opened with two teachers—Professor and Mrs. Brownsberger—and twenty-six students for a special eight-week term. From that beginning grew the nation's second-oldest Seventh-day Adventist college. By the end of the year there were six faculty members and a total of 152 students. The people of Healdsburg were pleased with both the faculty and students, and the success of the school seemed assured.

On October 2, 1882, a corporation was established with the college capitalized at $100,000. Stock was sold at ten dollars per share. At the incorporation meeting, 754 shares were subscribed by twenty-one people. Stock sales continued over the next two decades.

Education at Pacific Union College was seen as "improving the powers of the entire human organism," involving health, morals, and practical knowledge. Students were to attain a "commendable self-sufficiency" and be a "more profitable class of citizens," able to support themselves by some common means of livelihood. As a result of this posture, two and one half hours of manual labor were required daily. This apparently sharpened the students for their scholarly subjects and greatly improved their health. Professor Brownsberger was enthusiastic and stated: "We believe it is The Plan."

The town of Healdsburg began suffering financial problems compounded by the 1906 earthquake and urban development. As a result, on July 14, 1908, Pacific Union College closed its doors.

There were many months of searching and many disappointments before the right site became available for reestablishing Pacific Union College. After visiting the Angwin Resort on Howell Mountain, eight miles east of St. Helena, Ellen White decided that they should search no more. The dedication of Pacific College took place on September 29, 1909. In February of the following year it again became known as Pacific Union College, after the Pacific Union Conference assumed responsibility for the institution.

Today atop Howell Mountain, overlooking Napa Valley where the climate is mild and invigorating, sits the 2,000-acre campus with plenty of fresh air and acres of lush green woodlands. The 200-acre modern university now has sixty buildings.

The professors, all members of the Seventh-day Adventist Church, are still dedicated to the development of the whole being. The average enrollment at Pacific Union College is 1,400 students, approximately eleven students per teacher, which allows the faculty to take a personal interest in each student's progress.

Pacific Union College is a four-year liberal arts institution fully accredited by the Western Association of Schools and Colleges. The programs offered range from vocational to professional. Students leave the college as productive, well-balanced citizens, ready to assume their roles in the upper echelon of academic and professional occupations.

In addition, Pacific Union College offers a full-service airport, Virgil O.

Pacific Union College as it stands today on its 2,000-acre site atop Howell Mountain overlooking the beautiful Napa Valley.

Parrott Field, for the training of students as well as for public service. The institution also has become known for its cultural programs presented for the enjoyment of the surrounding communities. A recent addition to the college was the beautiful Austrian-built Rieger pipe organ, completed in 1981. It is the largest mechanical action organ on the West Coast.

Graduates of Pacific Union College have assumed significant positions of leadership throughout the world and offer testimony to the value of an integrated education of head, heart, and hand.

ST. HELENA HOSPITAL AND HEALTH CENTER

The original Adventist Health Retreat in 1892 in the quiet wooded foothills of Howell Mountain.

Seventh-day Adventists have been forerunners in developing excellent health care and nutritional programs. These programs are an outgrowth of the belief that optimum physical well-being parallels optimum spiritual health. Their preventive health programs developed in the 1800s were designed to help people discover optimum health or wellness, not just to recover from illness and disease.

It all began in 1866 on the edge of Battle Creek, Michigan, when the newly organized Seventh-day Adventist Church opened the doors of its first health care institution, the Western Health Reform Institute. Counsel on the principles used, in what has proven to be a sound philosophy of health, was received from Ellen G. White—a young Battlecreek housewife believed to be inspired by God. Many specific, practical instructions were revealed to her in 1863 and later. With these revelations as her guide, she combined in her own writings the best of both the orthodox physicians of her time and the

non-medically trained reformers and healers—thus developing the five principles of healthful living. These are balanced diet; natural remedies such as fresh air, sunshine, and water treatments; preventive medicine; mental health; and spiritual health.

With these early beginnings a young pioneer named Merritt G. Kellogg migrated by oxcart with his family in 1859 to California. (He was the half-brother of two world-famous Kelloggs—John Harvey of the Battle Creek Sanitarium and Will Keith of cornflake fame.) Even though he earned good wages in San Francisco as a carpenter, the young man felt he was not doing what God had designed for him. Therefore he sold his home, left his business, and returned east to enroll in Dr. Trall's Hygieo-Therapeutic College in New Jersey. After emerging six months later as a physician, he stated in a letter to Ellen White, "I did this because I believed the work of health reform was of God and that God had a work for me to do in the message."

Merritt Kellogg joined evangelists John Loughborough and D.T. Bordeau in California speaking on health subjects. In 1870 an epidemic of smallpox broke out while they were preaching in Bloomfield, a hamlet southwest of Santa Rosa. They immediately began treating the sick. A local physician lost four out of five patients, using drugs, while Kellogg saved ten out of eleven, using water treatments and healthful diets. After this Dr. Kellogg settled down to practice medicine in the village of Rutherford—four miles south of St. Helena—in the heart of what is now the Napa Valley wine-grape country. This brought him in touch with William A. Pratt, a retired bricklayer, and A.B. Atwood, a new convert to the Seventh-day Adventist Church. In 1877 Atwood became aware of the need for better medical facilities. The result was that he discussed this issue

with his friend Pratt and Dr. Kellogg, and the three men took action. Pratt donated ten acres of his land just 2.5 miles north of St. Helena, including an interest in Crystal Springs, and $3,000. Atwood furnished $1,000 and Kellogg promised $1,000 in labor. This was the beginning of the Rural Health Retreat operated in the West by Seventh-day Adventists.

Opening on June 7, 1878, with seven guests, the first building of the health retreat was a two-story structure, seventy-two by twenty-eight feet, with a thirteen-bed capacity. Within a year an addition had already been constructed. The institute was situated 400 feet above Napa Valley, which it immediately overlooked, and was surrounded by some of the most beautiful scenery in California.

The Rural Health Retreat became instrumental in developing the first tourist trade to Napa Valley as people traveled from far and near to view and partake of the "Rational Curative System," based on the theory that nature can provide its own remedies for all ailments to which the human body can succumb.

The institute maintained its own dairy, orchards, and vegetable gar-

The tree-lined path that guests were taken on as they approached the health retreat in 1895.

dens. Part of the early treatment and therapy was assigning a portion of the garden to a patient to care for, thus allowing him to recover his strength in the fresh air and sunshine while working with the soil.

Dr. Kellogg moved to Los Angeles in 1879—leaving "The Retreat" without a doctor for one year, during which time it operated as a health resort.

In 1884 Ellen White purchased 8.5 acres of adjacent land to be used for future development and built a three-story home, planned for institutional use. During the 1890s the retreat was renamed St. Helena Sanitarium. She remained in touch with the institution and led in counsel and in shaping such policies as natural methods of therapy, as opposed to drug therapy, and vegetarian, versus flesh, diets.

A school of nursing operated from 1891 to 1959 graduated 771 students. When the nursing program moved to Pacific Union College in nearby Angwin, the nurses' dorm was remodeled into Crystal Springs Manor—a 31-unit senior citizens' residence.

In 1907 Ellen White's foresight proved correct: The land she had held for twenty-three years was used to build a four-story hospital building, bringing it into a full acute-care hospital. The facility was then named St. Helena Sanitarium and Hospital.

The institution has continued to grow, and as an acute hospital it is today licensed for 165 inpatient beds and provides medical services for some twenty-five special fields of modern medical practice. It has gained a broad reputation for excellence as a center for cardiovascular services and a unique HEART (Health Education And Rehabilitation Training) program. This is a nineteen-day live-in cardiac conditioning plan designed to improve coronary health.

In 1969 the facility was renamed St. Helena Hospital and Health Cen-

The St. Helena Sanitarium as it appeared in 1906.

ter, and today has come full circle from preventive or wellness to acute care and back to include a "health center" that draws clients from all over the United States. It now offers a dozen live-in wellness programs such as alcoholism and chemical de-

An aerial view of the present-day St. Helena Hospital and Health Center.

pendency recovery, stress management, smoking cessation, weight management, cardiac, and eating disorders. Another service offered is a hospice program providing in-home care for the terminally ill—for which there is no direct charge to the patient. The institution has come a long way from the day it picked up its first visitors, in 1878, at the St. Helena train station with a team of horses and a buggy. Now transportation can be arranged from the San Francisco International Airport.

Today St. Helena Hospital and Health Center is one of the largest employers in the Napa Valley. Over 650 people are on the staff, including 100 physicians. This fully accredited facility is a member of the largest nonprofit hospital corporation in the nation, known as Adventist Health System/US, which is administered in a missionary spirit by the Seventh-day Adventist Church.

Ellen White wrote in 1903: "This institution was established by the Lord's direction and it is not to outlive its usefulness. It is to be a living institution, through which the light of truth shall be shed abroad."

NAPA VALLEY BANK

When a satisfied customer referred to Napa Valley Bank as "an oasis in the desert of the banking world," it was typical of the many favorable comments the institution has received over the years. Customers often write to express their appreciation for the exceptional personal service, concern, and consideration shown by Napa Valley Bank and its dedicated staff.

It's not surprising, since the institution was founded on the premise that personal service is key to banking success, and that a local bank is better able to achieve that commitment than the larger chain banks. Napa Valley Bank has not wavered from this principle in its fifteen years of operation. As founder and president Dale Kirkpatrick stated in a 1975 interview: "We are a Napa Valley institution. This is where we started, and this is where we'll stay."

Organization of Napa Valley Bank began on February 4, 1970, upon receiving formal approval from the State Banking Department. The bank was capitalized at $750,000 by issuing 50,000 shares of stock at $15 per share. A countywide public offering of the stock was made in the spring of 1970, with the sales initially re-stricted to local residents. It was felt that local ownership would ensure the bank's local orientation as it grew in the ensuing years.

After the formal approval was received, the institution's first board of directors was formed from several of the area's leading citizens. They included William P. Brooks, Dale Kirkpatrick, James A. Magetti, Dr. Dwight H. Murray, Jr., John A. Nemes, Earl Randol, and Robert H. Zeller. The board, representing a combined total of over 230 years' residence in the Napa Valley, formulated the policies of the new bank, and remained unchanged until Dale Kirkpatrick's retirement in 1984.

Kirkpatrick, named Napa Valley Bank's first president, had been president of Napa's El Dorado State Bank until it merged with United California Bank. A large part of his twenty-two years of banking experience, following his graduation from Kansas State University, had been with independent banks.

The site of Napa Valley Bank's first office was located in downtown Napa at the intersection of Clay, Polk, and Franklin streets. The bank was designed in the distinctive style of the California missions, a theme that has been continued in the construction of subsequent offices.

The first office was officially opened with a ribbon-cutting ceremony

This stained-glass window portraying the local scenery is part of the decor in the St. Helena Branch office.

on the morning of June 3, 1971. Thus, the only independent and locally owned bank in Napa County opened its doors for business. The vision of the founding directors had become a reality. And the community noticed the difference immediately. The bank's first innovation was the introduction of "people hours," extended banking hours for the convenience of its customers. Unlike the other banks of the time, Napa Valley Bank was (and remains today) open from 9 a.m. to 5 p.m. Monday through Thursday, 9 a.m. to 6 p.m. on Friday, and 9 a.m. to 1 p.m. on Saturday. However, the young financial institution was not immune to problems. The most memorable difficulty was a safe door that refused to budge just a few months after the bank opened. After reviewing the unpleasant alternatives, a professional "safecracker" was called in. He succeeded in freeing the door with the well-placed rap of a hammer.

The institution has grown dramatically over the years, becoming one of California's most successful and respected independent banks. Much of its success is attributed to Napa Valley Bank's dedication to personal service. Customers are greeted on a

The Trancas Street Branch, or the North Napa Branch, of Napa Valley Bank. Also shown is the Financial Plaza.

Bank directors and local dignitaries attend the June 1981 ribbon-cutting ceremonies at the Clay Street Branch.

first-name basis by staff members who, in most cases, have many years of service with the bank. Individuals are made to feel that their needs are important, and "people skills" rank high on the list of prerequisites for employment.

The concept of a locally owned community bank, oriented to the needs of local individuals and businesses, paid off immediately. Customers liked the fact that they were treated like neighbors, and that their deposits were kept in Napa County to be loaned out, as needed, to local individuals and commercial customers. Deposits and loans grew rapidly.

By the end of its first year, Napa Valley Bank was operating profitably, no small achievement for any new financial insitution. Traditionally slow starters, most banks do not show a profit until much later in their growth cycle. By the first year's end, Wanda Lamb became the first female officer of Napa Valley Bank with her promotion to assistant cashier in charge of operations and personnel. One of the institution's initial ten employees, she is still with Napa Valley Bank today.

Napa Valley Bank's first branch of-fice was opened in 1974 in Yountville. Gene Salazar, who remains with the bank today, was named the first manager of the office, which was also Yountville's first bank. The bank's next expansion came with the opening of its Calistoga office in 1975. Today there are seven offices in total, spanning the Napa Valley from American Canyon to Calistoga. Napa Valley Bank now has more offices in Napa County, and more automated teller machines, than any other bank. Further growth came recently with the formation of the Napa Valley De-

Steven I. Barlow, the second president of the Napa Valley Bank, assumed office in April 1984.

velopment Company, a wholly owned subsidiary.

On April 4, 1984, Steve Barlow became Napa Valley Bank's second president upon the retirement of Dale Kirkpatrick. He graduated from Stanford University in 1971 with a degree in economics. He joined Napa Valley Bank in 1975 as a loan officer, after four years with the Mechanics Bank of Richmond. In 1979 he was promoted to assistant vice-president, becoming a vice-president in 1981. In 1985 the bank added two new members to its board of directors: Edmond F. Brovelli, Jr., a native Napan, and Dana Leavitt.

Upon assuming the presidency of Napa Valley Bank, Steve Barlow stated his determination to maintain the bank's reputation for commitment to service and dedication to the local area. Under his leadership, the bank has continued its spectacular growth to become the second-largest bank operating in Napa County. Customers have continued to prosper as the bank introduced new services, expanded old ones, and offered aggressively competitive interest rates under provisions of federal banking deregulation.

Today Napa Valley Bank employs more than 190 local residents, with an annual payroll of over $4 million. By the close of 1985 assets had surpassed $190 million, with a net after-tax income of nearly $2 million.

In 1985 the bank formulated a new mission statement: "To maintain a dominant presence in our markets through effective and efficient delivery of quality banking services to individuals and businesses, while providing a balance of safety, yield, and growth that benefits our community, our employees, and our shareholders."

Despite its rapid growth, Napa Valley Bank has remained true to its founding principles, and is well-positioned to prosper for many years to come.

CROWN REALTY

Loyd D. Gularte's natural gift for salesmanship coupled with the management skills of his wife, Lovina, was apparently the making of a winning team. Together they have built a flourishing real estate business. When asked how he entered into real estate sales, Loyd responded: "I have been selling since the age of ten, beginning with magazines—the *Saturday Evening Post, Liberty* magazine—and that's all I have ever known. All my life I have been a salesman on a straight commission basis except for the three or four years I spent in the service and about three years working for a company in which my wife and I had an investment."

Loyd's sales career took him to the Walnut Creek area, where he met a construction sales manager for residential construction. He began his real estate sales career in Vallejo for the company that the sales manager represented.

In 1956 Loyd, a native Californian born in Petaluma, obtained his broker's license, and he and Lovina opened an office in Napa near Third and Franklin where he represented

contractors. While Loyd handled the sales, Lovina acted as office manager, bookkeeper, and janitor, as well as taking care of the children. According to Loyd, she was the "heart and soul" of the enterprise. Their children's exposure to the business at an early age was the beginning of a family operation.

This firm was sold, and for a year and a half Loyd worked for a mortgage company in Santa Rosa, helping it establish a real estate department. His roots were set in Napa by this time, however, and when he was asked by Harry E. Stover to join Stover Realty he accepted and returned to Napa to work. In 1962 they became partners. Harry retired a short time later and the Gulartes bought control of Stover Realty; several years later the name was changed

---

The Gularte family in front of their newest office complex, known as Gularte Plaza and located at 3404 Valle Verde. Seated are Lovina and Loyd Gularte and standing (left to right) are Crystal and Randy Gularte and Dave and Sharii Carmichael. Sharii is the daughter of Loyd and Lovina Gularte.

to Crown Realty. At this time it was located on Clay Street.

With urban development becoming a reality and it becoming more and more obvious that the city was going to move north, a house was purchased at 1155 Trancas. Later it was remodeled into a commercial office building and won the Napa Chamber of Commerce award for finest remodeling for commercial use. This structure became the firm's new office. As the Gulartes' business grew, the children grew—and their son, Randy, obtained his real estate license at the age of eighteen. The family became involved in community affairs and organizations. Randy went on to graduate from Cal State Sacramento with a major in real estate and business administration, and two months after graduation obtained his broker's license. With Randy through school and looking to the future growth of the business, the family decided to incorporate. The firm became Loyd D. Gularte, Inc., with Randy as president; Lovina, secretary/treasurer; and Loyd, chairman of the board. They jointly agreed to build what is now Gularte Plaza at 3404 Valle Verde, which also won a chamber of commerce award. In 1980 the Gulartes moved their office into one building and leased the other side. Presently they have twenty-six sales people working with them and preparations are now being made to expand their operation into the second building. The Gulartes' daughter, Sharii Carmichael, and three of four other office personnel cover the clerical and administrative affairs of the business. With the new generation moving into positions of responsibility, it appears that Crown Realty's goals—to treat everyone fairly and equally; to be sure the family fits the home, and the home fits the family; and to give back to the community what the community gives to you—have remained the same.

BELL PRODUCTS, INC.

A business-minded artist and crafts-man with a vision for the future is a rare combination indeed. All of these qualities were apparently possessed by Joe Bell, the founder of Bell Products, Inc.

Bell was formerly employed at Mare Island as a sheet metal worker until 1945. After the war he established Bell Products in an old wagon wheel barn at 2325 First Street in Napa. The entrepreneur had rare ability, according to the inscription on a plaque presented to him by his employees in 1978. He began the business as a sign maker, as well as fabricating other sheet metal products. He prided himself in providing state-of-the-art products. This was evident as photographs, which had been taken over the years, were viewed of his completed projects. Another element responsible for his business growth was that of extending superior service. Excellence was his trademark.

At the end of its first year, the firm had three employees. Its business continued to grow with postwar remodeling jobs of many storefronts in Napa; and then began pioneering in the heating and air-conditioning

Walt Blackmon, vice-president and commercial field manager, has been with Bell Products, Inc., since 1957.

Jim Asbury, president, started with the firm in 1961 and is now general manager.

construction industry, remaining a leader in this field. With Bell's vision for the future, he was open to using innovative ideas that were in keeping with his standards of excellence. It was he who was responsible for the introduction of perimeter heating to Napa.

Bell Products, Inc., has done installations in many businesses and institutions in Napa, Solano, Alameda, Contra Costa, Marin, Sonoma, Lake, and many other surrounding counties. The list of satisfied customers is long. In order to service this clientele, a need was created to build a work force of equally dedicated employees with a commitment to service, quality, and integrity.

Many apprentices have become indentured to Bell Products, Inc., through the Sheet Metal Workers' Union. Not only do they learn the trade, a commitment to excellence is imparted to them as well. Once the apprentices attain journeyman status, many will stay on—but whether they stay or move on, there is no question they have been well trained not only as craftsman but also in the areas of service and integrity.

The company was incorporated in 1957, and presently employs fifty-five

people. Thirty-five are sheet metal workers. The current owners are Walt Blackmon, commercial field manager; Jim Asbury, general manager; and Bob Winchell, light commercial and residential manager. They have eighty-five combined years of service.

Bell Products, Inc., has been at the present location, 722 Soscol, since 1964. Today its primary capabilities are heating and air conditioning, sheet metal and custom fabrication, and service and repair. In keeping with the founder's vision of innovative methods, the fabricating shop has increased its production with the introduction of a computerized plasma cutter. The firm is keeping abreast of the latest in equipment and production.

The present staff of administrative personnel, estimators and sales people, and detailers and technicians are trained to serve the community and are concerned with the betterment of Napa. These standards have not changed and are in recognition of Joe Bell, who started in an old wagon-wheel barn in 1945. With rare ability and his own hands, he built the present Bell Products, Inc.

Bob Winchell has been with Bell Products, Inc., since 1955 and is now secretary/treasurer and residential field manager.

125

NAPA VALLEY LODGE

In the aloha spirit a pineapple, the Hawaiian symbol of hospitality, stands at the heart of a lovely fountain imported from Italy. Located at the center of the colorful tile-covered entry to Napa Valley Lodge, this fountain symbolizes the hospitality and service that awaits guests as they step over the threshold.

Situated on a piece of land at the northern edge of Yountville and backing up to Highway 29 sits a picturesque California mission-style lodge. Across the street is a quiet tree-shaded community park, which adds to the feeling of warmth and hospitality. Sitting against a backdrop of vineyards and tree-studed hills, Napa Valley Lodge could be reminiscent of an early resort.

Even though Napa Valley Lodge has a relatively brief history, it may be considered a pioneer in its field. In the early 1970s, when Napa Valley was beginning to gain world prominence for its wine production and the tourist trade was developing, there were no full-service lodges in the valley. Responding to the need, the Napa Valley Lodge opened in March 1978 as a mom-and-pop operation, with an eye to future expansion.

Since that time the lodge has expanded its services to meet the needs of its growing clientele. However, from the start service and hospitality have been first and foremost in its operation, and as the lodge has grown it has not wavered in this commitment.

At present there are fifty-five rooms, including four fully equipped conference rooms that can accommodate either business or social functions. In July 1985 the Vintage Hall Conference Complex was opened. Complete with an imported fireplace from Italy that graces the main conference room, the complex opens onto the pool and courtyard area, creating an ideal setting for recep-

tions, reunions, and business meetings. The grand opening took place in November 1985, with a post-theater party hosted by Napa Valley Lodge and Beringer Winery for the Napa Valley Symphony. It was a gala affair with approximately 150 people in attendance.

In addition to the conference room, there is also a full exercise and weight room, a sauna, a poolside spa, and an extra-large swimming pool. These facilities enable guests to continue their exercise programs without interruption.

With the numerous amenities available to guests, the present-day lodge is not unlike its counterpart of the resort era. Napa Valley Lodge

The Napa Valley Lodge, winner of the AAA Four Diamond Award for Exceptional Lodging Standards.

offers large guest rooms that open out onto private balconies overlooking the valley. Some rooms have tile Mediterranean-style fireplaces. A complimentary continental breakfast is served each morning. Weather permitting, it is served around the pool in the courtyard area. Catered meals are available upon request and the town of Yountville offers a number of select restaurants, all within easy walking distance of the lodge. Bicycles are available for guests who wish to tour the countryside and take in the rich

splendor of the valley. Our modern-day society is more mobile and the average length of stay is shorter, but the service and hospitality provided by the Napa Valley Lodge encourage a rate of return much the same as the early resorts.

For the convenience of the business and professional community wishing to conduct meetings or seminars in a more relaxed atmosphere away from the corporate setting, fully equipped conference rooms are available, complete with podiums and audiovisual equipment. Service is tailored to the specific needs of each group.

The occupancy rate of the Napa Valley Lodge has been 100 percent, and the staff operates as efficiently as a well-oiled machine. At the height

of the season, operating the facility requires a staff of twenty-five.

Napa Valley Lodge was founded by Ellis Alden, a former attorney who was educated at Dartmouth College before coming to the San Francisco area. Napa Valley Lodge is the third such facility founded by its owner and one of five full-service lodges and hotels that fall under the umbrella of the Western Lodging Management Company, with corporate offices in Redwood City. Each lodge and hotel operates as a separate entity, with its own administrative staff that makes decisions on the local level.

Alden's first facility was the Bodega Bay Lodge, in 1972. Alden, a spontaneous young man with foresight, came upon the Bodega Bay Motel

Among its many amenities, the lodge boasts a poolside spa and an extra-large swimming pool.

while out for a weekend drive. When he discovered it was for sale, he decided to purchase it. Putting his creative skills to work, Alden rebuilt the facility into an oceanside luxury lodge. After that came the Half Moon Bay Lodge in 1976, followed by the Napa Valley Lodge two years later.

More recently, in June 1984 the Stanford Park Hotel was opened in Menlo Park. Scheduled for opening in June 1986 is the Lafayette Park Hotel in Lafayette. Each facility is unique in styling and affords all the modern comforts available. They are reflective of an extremely gifted and creative businessman.

HANNS KORNELL CHAMPAGNE CELLARS

Hanns Kornell entered the United States as an emigrant from Nazi Germany, but he is quick to state that he was a "newcomer" and not a refugee. He came as a highly skilled craftsman trained as a champagne master by his father, grandfather, and uncle, renowned in Europe for their prize champagne.

The young man was moving into his career and beginning to establish his own reputation when World War II broke out; and in 1938 Kornell, who is Jewish, spent some time in a German concentration camp at Dachau. Upon his release from Dachau he fled to England where he found work as a bottle washer, after convincing a judge that he was a friendly

Hanns Kornell at work in his famous champagne cellar.

alien. After working there for a year, until 1940, he had saved enough money to travel on to the United States.

Kornell was determined to reestablish his career, in America, as a champagne master. Unable to find work in New York, and with only two dollars left of his savings, he began hitchhiking to California—the land of promise—where he initially obtained employment in a service station, which was soon followed by a position as a champagne maker. After working for a time at Fountain Grove Vineyard in Santa Rosa, Kornell went east and made champagne for the Gibson Wine Company in Cincinnati and Kentucky. From there he moved on to St. Louis, where he made Cook's Imperial Champagne for the American Wine Company.

Hanns Kornell, founder, in earlier days.

Finally able to save enough to establish his own business, in 1952 Kornell returned to California with his savings and a $3,000 loan from a friend. He leased a small winery, in the county of Sonoma, for $100 a month—where he was assisted by one employee. Bottling was done at night, and during the day the entrepreneur peddled his product door to door from his panel truck. He relates an early marketing technique used in trying to get his champagne into the Mark Hopkins Hotel. The winegrower told the proprietor his champagne would keep its bubbles for one month after being opened. "He didn't believe me, so we compared with a one-month test." Two glasses were poured, one each from a Kornell bottle and the hotel brand. The bottles were recorked and refrigerated for thirty days. Upon reopening, the Kornell champagne frothed out of the bottle; the other was flat. "This got me into the Mark Hopkins, and I've been there for twenty-five years."

The winery's superb champagnes are produced by the traditional Methode Champenoise, a process originated in the Champagne region of France, in which the champagne is bottled, fermented, aged, and

Hanns Kornell and his wife, Marilouise, with their children, Paula and Peter, and friend, Polo, as they relax in front of their historic stone aging vaults, which were originally the Larkmead Winery.

shipped in the original bottle. The Hanns Kornell labels read proudly, "Naturally fermented in this bottle." This method, handed down through three generations, is utilized as a foundation for superb quality.

The symbol of the Israelites carrying a huge cluster of grapes on a branch between them is found on every bottle of Hanns Kornell Champagne. The scouts of the biblical story brought with them the finest quality grapes found in Canaan, the land of promise. Quality is also emphasized at Hanns Kornell. The cellars are located in one of the most fertile valleys of the world, where every year there is the promise of great quality wines—the finest of which are used to make Hanns Kornell Champagne.

This ideal location, four miles north of St. Helena in the heart of Napa Valley wine country, was purchased in 1958. The massive stone and timber cellars, designed and built by Wilbur Harrison in 1906, were originally the Larkmead Winery. Considered one of the finest structures in the area, it has been added to the National Register of Historic Places.

Producing one million bottles of champagne in 1985, the Kornell winery has won awards all over the world for the past thirty years. The founder's wife, Marilouise, and their two children, Paula and Peter, have been very much involved in the champagne production. A $6-million offer for the winery from a Japanese steel company was refused. "We eat with it and sleep with it; this is our life," states the founder. Paula is now vice-president and director of marketing and sales; Peter, presently attending Fresno State University, is active in the winery and public relations. Hanns and Marilouise are both from long lines of wine makers—Hanns traces his own wine-maker roots back to 1780.

Hanns Kornell has come a long way from the young immigrant hitchhiking to the promised land with only two dollars in his pocket. Today the family lives in a lovely setting, with ample space for their beautiful horses and dogs. They have traveled worldwide marketing their champagne, winning many awards. The winegrower states: "I get tired, but I will not retire. I get up in the morning and feed the horses and dogs and come to the winery to work. This is my life." He has accomplished much in his lifetime to be proud of—and much that he has perpetuated will live on in generations to come.

A bottle of Hanns Kornell Champagne with the famous label—two men of Caanan carrying a grape cluster on a pole.

QUEEN OF THE VALLEY HOSPITAL

Before there was a hospital in Napa, people needing surgery or urgent medical attention had to endure a buggy ride over bumpy roads to Vallejo or be transported to San Francisco by steamer.

Napa's first hospital was founded in 1910 by three prominent physicians, Drs. Lawrence Welti, M.L. Daugherty, and E.Z. Hennessey. The local physicians named their fifteen-bed facility the Benjamin Shurtleff Hospital.

A second privately owned institution, known as Francis Hospital, was established in 1919 by Dr. Charles Bulson. He later took into partnership Drs. Dwight H. Murray and Hubert Coleman. It was a 24-bed hospital with a surgery area, a delivery room, and a nursery, located at Jefferson and Calistoga streets.

It became more and more evident that a community hospital was needed. The small, privately owned facilities were not adequate and could not keep up economically with the growing community. Local businessmen and doctors joined together to establish a community hospital. A site was located at the corner of G and Jefferson streets, and it was agreed that the community hospital would be called Victory Hospital. It was ready to receive its first patients in 1929. The medical staff consisted of nine physicians, all the members of the County Medical Society who were practicing in Napa at the time.

The institution was later renamed Parks Victory Hospital for Anna Parks, longtime superintendent of the hospital. In 1946 the facility was restructured and set up as a nonprofit organization under the laws of the State of California. It then became known as Parks Victory Memorial Hospital.

The institution grew rapidly in the years that followed, soon increasing its bed capacity from thirty-five to forty-five. After the war the expanding community came to realize that the facility was no longer adequate. It also became evident that the growing institution needed consistent administration. It was suggested that a religious order, experienced in hospital management, might be interested in assuming the administration of Parks

Sister Ann McGuinn, C.S.J., present administrator of the Queen of the Valley Hospital, standing in front of the original building.

Victory Memorial Hospital.

That proposal was met with opposition. Some were skeptical about turning a nonprofit community hospital over to a religious order. However, after considerable discussion, followed by a town meeting explaining the proposal, an agreement was reached to turn the administration of the hospital over to the religious order.

On May 1, 1953, the Sisters of St. Joseph assumed responsibility for the 45-bed Parks Victory Memorial Hospital with the commitment to maintain it as a community hospital. They also pledged to build a new and larger facility within five years.

Queen of the Valley Hospital has evolved into not only an acute care facility, but the major diagnostic and therapeutic center for the region.

Sister Bernadette McKeown, shortly before she passed away in March 1986.

THE SISTERS OF ST. JOSEPH

The Sisters of St. Joseph of Orange are a Catholic order of women committed to being a bonding force between Christ and the community. They are dedicated to improving the quality of life for the poor and suffering in the name of Christ, especially in the fields of education, health care, and social services.

The order was founded in France in 1651 by Jean Pierre Medaille to bring unity and reconciliation to the people. Their work was interrupted by the French Revolution in 1789, but was reestablished in 1806. The first American branch of the order was organized in 1836, and the Sisters began serving the unique needs of frontier America. The order was established in California in 1912, and this branch became known as the Sisters of St. Joseph of Orange in 1922, when they established their headquarters in that city.

Having established a reputation in California for successful hospital administration, the Sisters of St. Joseph of Orange were chosen to run Parks Victory Memorial Hospital. Mother Francis Lirette, Sister M. Paul Schwickerath, and Sister Bernadette McKeown were the pioneer group who came to Napa to give leadership to the hospital. Mother Francis became chairman of the hospital's board of directors, Sister M. Paul was named director of nursing, and Sister Bernadette became hospital administrator.

The Sisters were dynamic and true to their word in that they immediately began planning for the new fa-

cility. Their spirituality, coupled with their intellectual and social skills, proved to be a great asset to the Napa community. The Sisters assured the community that the hospital would be maintained as a community-oriented institution. That proved to be the key to the success of their fund-raising efforts.

It was through these efforts that Sister Bernadette became endeared to the community. She worked closely with many of Napa's civic leaders and won the respect of all who came in contact with her. She seemed to have the ability to relate to everyone. Sister Bernadette proved to be an as-

tute businesswoman and, with the support of Mother Francis and Sister M. Paul, the dream of a modern community hospital was brought to fruition. She was the bonding force drawing the community together.

On March 5, 1958, a new 96-bed institution named Queen of the Valley opened its doors to a new era of hospital care.

The officers of the Queen of the Valley Foundation, when the charter was signed in October 1969, were (left to right) foundation president Karney Kenchelian, secretary Eloise Rota, and treasurer Walter Fogerty, Sr.

(Left to right) R. Michael Mondavi, president of Queen of the Valley Foundation; Sue Fogerty, president of Community Projects; and Pedi the bear present the first installment of a $125,000 pledge for the pediatrics department to Sister Ann McGuinn, hospital administrator.

NAPA VALLEY MEDICAL CENTER

Queen of the Valley Hospital was founded by the Sisters of St. Joseph. They assumed leadership of the old Parks Victory Hospital on May 1, 1953, with a five-year plan for a new facility. On March 5, 1958, the new 96-bed hospital was opened at 1000 Trancas Street in Napa.

A successful drive to raise funds for the new hospital was directed by some of Napa's civic leaders and resulted in the initial ground breaking in 1955. That was the beginning of the bonding between Napa citizens and the hospital. This relationship, encouraged by the Sisters, has brought Queen of the Valley Hospital into a new era of health care as not only an acute care facility, but also as the major diagnostic and therapeutic center for the region. Its location in the Napa Valley, the support of the community, and the institution's ability to deliver quality medical care with state-of-the-art equipment have been chiefly responsible for attracting dedicated, high-caliber physicians.

In 1965 Sister Jean Therese Bevans was named administrator. Her leadership brought about further growth in the hospital to meet the needs of the valley.

By the hospital's tenth anniversary in 1968 many changes had taken place. In 1962 a four-bed intensive care unit was opened. Two years later the north wing was added, increasing hospital capacity to 135 beds. A third X-ray room, a laboratory, and a pediatrics department also were added. The year 1968 brought EEG testing. That year total admissions were 5,523.

Sister Ann McGuinn assumed leadership at Queen of the Valley in 1971. Her goals at that time were to update the services that were being provided and also to provide services for which Napa Valley residents had to travel outside the community.

By the institution's twentieth anniversary the new west wing had been constructed. Added services included kidney dialysis, mammography, cardiac monitors, a linear accelerator, and a CT scanner. During that period assets increased to seventeen million dollars, with 25 percent directly attributed to equipment.

As the Queen of the Valley Hospital approaches her thirtieth anniversary more expansion has taken place. Ground-breaking ceremonies for the $13.5-million nursing pavilion took

Edmond F. Brovelli Sr., former president of the Queen of the Valley board of trustees and prominent community leader; Sister Ann McGuinn, C.S.J., hospital administrator; and Marion Weitz, M.D., at one of the many ground-breaking ceremonies heralding hospital expansion. Brovelli passed away at his home on April 5, 1986, at the age of eighty-two.

place on February 14, 1983, just before the institution's twenty-fifth anniversary. The nursing pavilion was dedicated May 17, 1985, replacing all previous patient areas with modern, efficient private and semiprivate rooms complete with built-in monitoring equipment providing the most up-to-date patient care. Total capacity has been increased to 180 beds.

In 1981 the Sisters of St. Joseph organized their eight hospitals into a health system enabling the institutions to better address future challenges being brought about by the changes in the delivery of health care. At the same time the philosophy was reaffirmed, emphasizing the purpose and mission of the Sisters of St. Joseph in health care: to promote Christian community and enhance the dignity of persons in the care of the whole person, body, mind, and soul, as an extension of Christ's mission of mercy to his people.

QUEEN OF THE VALLEY HOSPITAL FOUNDATION

In the 1980s the Queen of the Valley Hospital's dedication to its most important partner, the community, has been intensified, and together they have built a multimillion-dollar medical center. This dedication has been carried out, in part, by the Queen of the Valley Foundation.

Incorporated as a separate non-profit community trust in 1969 by Napa community leaders, the foundation has been unswerving in its efforts to assist the hospital in securing the equipment and developing the programs necessary to meet the health care needs of the Napa Valley. While raising money remains a primary function, the organization is also deeply involved in determining community health care needs and in enlisting public interest, action, and support of hospital projects.

The Queen of the Valley Foundation is set up to accept gifts of cash, securities, and real estate on behalf of the hospital. Contributions may be made to mark special occasions or in memory of a loved one. In addition to receiving gifts on behalf of the hospital, the organization is actively engaged in specific fund-raising efforts. Among these are the annual A Day for the Queen at the Silverado Country Club, the Designers' Showhouse, and the Dr. Dwight H. Murray, Sr., Golf and Tennis Tournament.

Napa Valley Vintners' Napa Valley Wine Auction serves as a fund raiser for the health care facilities in Napa County. Since 1981 Queen of the Valley Hospital Foundation has been the recipient of $367,000 from this effort.

The Queen of the Valley Foundation raised $1.7 million in funds to outfit the hospital's emergency department and intensive care unit with state-of-the-art monitoring equipment for critically ill patients. Also purchased were a digital angiography system to pinpoint circulatory ailments and a linear accelerator to provide modern radiation therapy for the treatment of cancer.

The most recent fund-raising campaign has brought in the required $2.5 million necessary to equip and furnish the recently completed nursing pavilion.

Virginia Simms, longtime supporter of the Queen of the Valley Hospital and member of the hospital foundation, with the Most Reverend Mark J. Hurley, D.D., Ph.D., of the Diocese of Santa Rosa. Bishop Hurley blessed the new nursing pavilion at dedication ceremonies on May 17, 1985.

Sisters Ann McGuinn, C.S.J.; Elaine Moffette, C.S.J.; Rose Mary Green, C.S.J.; Mary Louise Simonot, C.S.J.; Kathleen Small, C.S.J.; and Peggy Detert, C.S.J., being presented Valentine's Day bouquets by Lucas Lies before the ground-breaking ceremonies for the new nursing pavilion on February 14, 1983.

KVON/KVYN RADIO

On November 22, 1946, an application was filed with the FCC to give Napa its first radio station. The power would be 500 watts. It stated that the population of Napa was 7,740, of the county, 28,503. Two years later the application was granted, and Elwyn F. Quinn became the first general manager of Napa Broadcasting Company and KVON, "the Voice of Napa." Luther Gibson and the *Vallejo Times* were the next owners, followed by a well-known network radio announcer, Fort Pearson. Pearson sold to Jack Powell, who operated the facility for eight years. Powell sold to Larry Scheer and Janice Lynn. Scheer was a popular air personality in the Los Angeles area. Three years later Art Youngberg purchased KVON and sold to Young Radio Inc., Tom Young, president. That was the fall of 1970. In twenty-two years KVON had six owners; there has been just one in the sixteen years since, but the power has increased ten times from 500 watts to 5,000, and from one radio station to two.

In 1972 Young Radio, Inc., began Napa's first and only television station. A studio was built at 1124 Foster Road, the same location of KVON. TV-6 provided cable subscribers with nightly news and local sporting events. In 1975 Young Radio discontinued operation of TV-6 in order to use the studios for its new radio station, KVYN, Napa Valley's first FM station.

In 1976 KVYN's eighty-foot tower was erected on the 1,200-foot hill near Ernest Ilsley's property on Silverado Trail, east of Yountville. The transmitter has been out of service for only two days since 1976. That outage occurred when it was destroyed by the fire of 1982. However, during the flood of 1986 it was the only source of radio communication for local residents. KVYN operated as a public service for area residents and flood victims, without the benefit of advertising during that disaster.

The AM station, KVON, has been housed at 1124 Foster Road since 1948. Its four 200-foot towers were located on the Foster Road site from 1948 until 1985, when they were moved near the campus of Napa Valley College next to the Napa River. The only time the station was not in

Tom Young, president of Young Radio, Inc., and owner of KVON/KVYN since 1971.

service was a day and a half during the flood of 1986, when the transmitter was flooded with five feet of water.

As the community has grown and the market has expanded, Young Radio, Inc., has increased its staff from seven employees in 1970 to thirty in 1986. Tom Young has been a leader in his profession at the local, state, and national levels. He was president of the Minnesota and Iowa state broadcasting associations, and is a member of the board of directors of the National Association of Broadcasters in Washington, D.C. He states that he enjoys every day in his chosen profession, and the years in the valley have been most enjoyable.

Young has always encouraged his staff to be civic leaders as well. Jay Goetting, a twelve-year veteran news editor of KVON/KVYN, is a Napa County supervisor. George Carl, vice-president/general sales manager since 1968, is a leader in the world of the "outdoorsman." Millie Voyles, office manager since 1958, is president of the Women's Division of the Chamber of Commerce, and past president of the Soroptomist Club.

Under the ownership of Young Radio, Inc., KVON and KVYN have truly become "the Voices of the Napa Valley."

KVON and TV 6 Broadcast Park after the new studios were built.

BROADCAST PARK
KVON 1440 · CABLE TV 6

SLINSEN CONSTRUCTION COMPANY

In 1987 Slinsen Construction Company will celebrate its fiftieth anniversary of service to Napa County. The expansion from a 1928 caterpillar tractor to a fleet of fifty-six pieces of heavy equipment, consuming several thousand gallons of fuel each month and requiring a radio communication system to keep in contact during the busy season, is visible proof that the company has grown with the community.

George Slinsen—a native Napan, born on Mount Veeder, and a rancher—began the enterprise in 1937, hiring himself and his tractor out to other ranchers to work the ground in their orchards. (During that era Napa Valley was primarily prune, cherry, and walnut orchards.) As time went on, more equipment and operators were added; and Slinsen's role in Napa development began to grow: He went from vineyard and orchard work to paving and engineering. One of his first major contracts was the East Side Reservoir, for the City of Napa, on Monez Boulevard. In the 1950s he built the first Silverado golf course and subsequently the club's tennis courts were done; the Kennedy golf course was another project undertaken. The site work (grading and

The Old Sonoma Road overpass job was done in 1961 by Slinsen Construction Company.

paving) was done for Napa and Vintage high schools. Many of the developments or subdivisions in Napa were contracted to Slinsen Construction Company, which completed the grading, paving, curb, and gutter projects. When the orchards were replanted into vineyards, the firm did much of the clearing and soil preparation. As Napa Valley came more to be known as the "Wine Country," and wineries began to grace the landscape, Slinsen Construction again was on the job—accomplishing the site work for Trefethan Vineyards, Robert Mondavi Winery, Franciscan Winery, and Domaine Chandon. The Robert Mondavi home was a later project. State highway endeavors were also effected; an important example is the Old Sonoma Road overpass and access roads, completed in 1961.

In 1954 Slinsen's son-in-law, Kenneth Tronstad, joined the organization as an operator. After a two-year interruption to serve in the Army, from 1955 to 1957, the young man returned to that position. As the company grew he assumed more responsibility.

The company's first office was located on Trancas Street, situated where Long's Drugs now stands. Ironically, Slinsen Construction did the site work for its successor's shopping complex.

In 1977 the firm was incorporated. The following year George Slinsen became ill, and Tronstad then became general manager. Purchasing the company in 1981, after the found-

er's death, he has continued to operate under the same philosophy as his father-in-law: "to do the best job possible, and to always treat the customer with complete integrity."

The office presently stands on a five-acre site at 1314 McKinstry Street. A full-time mechanic is maintained year-round, and during the busy season as many as twenty-five people are employed—some of whom have been with the corporation for as long as thirty years. An outstanding safety record has been maintained, with many safety awards won.

Slinsen Construction Company has played a major role in the development of Napa County, and many projects will remain and serve as a memorial to George Slinsen, its founder.

Kenneth Tronstad purchased the company in 1981 after the death of his father-in-law, George Slinsen. Here he is shown in the present office at 1314 McKinstry Street.

George Slinsen, founder of Slinsen Construction Company, on his Napa Valley ranch.

NAPA STATE HOSPITAL

Imola, a city unto itself when it was established in the late 1800s, was not unlike its Italian counterpart. (Imola, Italy, is located twenty-one miles southeast of Bologna on the Santerno near a fertile plain, where there stood a communal palace with nearby mineral springs, factories, and spinning mills.)

Edmund T. Wilkins, M.D., a native of Montgomery County, Tennessee, arrived in San Francisco on January 26, 1852. After receiving his medical diploma Dr. Wilkins, a longtime resident farmer in Butte County, moved to Marysville in July 1861. There he practiced medicine, concentrating his efforts on the care and treatment of the mentally ill.

The first state hospital for the mentally ill was constructed in Stockton in 1852. It was built to accommodate eighty persons, and by the late 1860s had become vastly overcrowded. In 1870 the state legislature passed a bill to take steps to establish a second state hospital. Governor

Dr. Edmund T. Wilkins, one of the hospital's founders, was superintendent from March 1876 to February 1891.

H.H. Haight commissioned Dr. Wilkins to conduct a study of other institutions in order to implement the best possible design and plan for the care and treatment of the mentally ill.

Dr. Wilkins traveled throughout North America and Europe studying 149 institutions. He returned to California and made an exhaustive report favoring the "moral treatment" of the mentally ill, and presented it to the governor of California on December 2, 1871. After reviewing the report, the state legislature approved an act to build a second state hospital.

Governor Booth appointed three commissioners who would select a site and location for the new facility. They were Dr. Wilkins; Dr. George A. Shurtleff, superintendent of the Stockton state hospital; and Judge C.H. Swift of Sacramento.

Napa was selected as the site of the new hospital because of its healthful and stable climate, the fact that it offered good land at reasonable rates, and its nearness to a waterway for receiving supplies. Three Napa pioneers were appointed to the board of directors. They were James Goodman, a banker; Chancellor Hartson, a lawyer; and Robert Sterling, a businessman and county official. They were to administer the funds to build the 500-bed hospital.

The board of directors first purchased 192 acres of land from Don Cayetano Juarez. Later additional land was acquired, bringing the total area to more than 2,000 acres. The area included a wharf on the Napa River, a siding at the Southern Pacific tracks, vegetable fields, a duck ranch, and the Skyline Park area. An outlying ranch, bounded by Coombsville and Green Valley roads, provided the hospital's main source of water. Cattle was raised on the Napa State Hospital Farm just northeast of Yountville and provided beef for the Napa State Asylum, the Veterans Home of California, and San Quentin.

The architectural contract was awarded to the San Francisco firm of Wright and Sanders. In October 1872 ground was broken for the new facility, and actual construction be-

Rear view of the hospital in its early days. The sea of white in the foreground is the laundry hanging out to dry.

A second California state hospital for the mentally ill was proposed, and Napa, with its healthful climate, was chosen as the site. The domestic Gothic structure was dedicated December 24, 1874.

The hospital was almost totally self-sufficient with its own vegetable gardens and the Napa State Hospital Farm northeast of Yountville, a beef cattle operation that provided meat for Napa State Hospital, the Veterans Home of California, and San Quentin.

gan February 11, 1873. the cornerstone was laid and the building was dedicated December 24, 1874. The brick and stone used in the construction of the hospital were supplied from a quarry on the grounds.

The seven-towered domestic Gothic structure was elaborate and ornate, and its uniqueness made it one of Napa's early tourist attractions. The hospital faced the west with wings extending on either side, allowing for plenty of fresh air to flow throughout the facility. There was an underground cog railroad used to carry meals and laundry to the hospital's wings.

The first patients were admitted November 15, 1875—the average stay being about three months. Many of the patients were displaced persons or suffered from alcoholism or drug addiction. By 1880 the patient load had increased to such an extent that funds were appropriated to finish the attic areas to accommodate more residents.

The Napa State Asylum soon became self-sufficient. A prize-winning dairy herd was developed, vegetable gardens and orchards abounded, and the facility had its own bakery.

On March 16, 1876, Dr. Wilkins became resident physician of the Napa State Asylum, succeeding Dr. Edward Bentley. The hospital ran smoothly and efficiently under Dr. Wilkins' administration. The occupational therapy programs proved successful, and the fresh air and outdoor environment seemed to have healing powers.

In 1922 the Department of Institutions was established. Under this department's direction viewpoints changed about mental illness. The name of the facility was changed to Napa State Hospital, and the term "insanity" became recognized as "mental illness."

In addition, the old structure became outdated. It was demolished in 1949 and replaced by more modern facilities. In January 1984 another major remodeling progam was undertaken.

Overcrowded conditions have existed throughout the history of the hospital. The peak period came in 1960, when 4,991 patients were housed at the facility. After 1960 admissions began to decline as changes took place in government levels of responsibility, and more county- and regional-based programs were developed.

A standard of moral treatment was established from the earliest days of the hospital, with occupational therapy programs and exercise classes part of the treatment.

Today the executive director has full authority for the operation of the facility and is presently working under the direction of two government agencies: the State Department of Developmentally Disabled and the State Department of Mental Health. The Napa State Hospital now offers eleven treatment programs for the developmentally and mentally disabled.

VETERANS HOME OF CALIFORNIA

Another group that chose Napa Valley as the site for establishing an institution because of its healthful and tranquil atmosphere was the founders of the Veterans Home of California in Yountville. The facility celebrated its centennial in 1984, marking 100 years of providing the "Good Life" for California veterans. With its second century came the endorsement of the Master Plan, a long-range project for remodeling and expansion of the entire facility that will take it into the twenty-first century. Thus, the home's first 100 years have laid the groundwork for a successful future.

When the Veterans Home of California opened its doors on April 1, 1884, to its first residents, it was still under the auspices of a private corporation that was long on humanitarianism and short of capital. The group was continually looking for support from private veterans' groups

A $53-million plan for renovation of the entire Veterans Home is under way. Wilson Hall is typical of the beautiful old buildings in the early California style that will be rehabilitated for semiprivate and private rooms, air conditioning, and handicapped access.

and from the government.

The need for a care and support group for a growing population of disabled veterans in California became a matter of concern to the San Francisco chapter of the Grand Army of the Republic (GAR). In 1877 a committee was established to undertake a study of the situation and determine what could be done to correct it. Growing out of this study was the idea of a home for disabled veterans. That idea was endorsed by the California Department of the GAR and the Associated Veterans of the Mexican War. The committee immediately incorporated and established the Veterans Home Association. Fund-raising campaigns were launched, and the first effort brought in $20,000. Of that amount, $17,300 was used to purchase 910 acres of land near Yountville, "a rural paradise."

Public interest developed, and many fund-raising campaigns later,

Armistice Chapel, built in 1918, has been fully restored and is the home of the California Veterans Museum.

the association finally had enough money to begin construction. The first building was a frame structure. Named the Grand Mark Administration Building, it served the home for sixty years.

Financial problems were ongoing; however, the home's population continued to grow. It became partially self-supporting with its agricultural and livestock operations and resident work programs. The veterans helped build their community in whatever way they could. The association struggled to keep the home in operation, and through its efforts more buildings were added and the facility continued to grow. By 1897 it was valued at $320,000.

The Veterans Home of California was growing so rapidly that the financial burden became overwhelming. Both veterans groups agreed to dissolve the corporation and deed the property over to the State of California as a gift. The property consisted of fifty-five buildings, housing some 800 veterans. The State of California has maintained the home since 1897.

Today the facility is operated on an annual budget of close to forty million dollars in a unique partnership between the state and federal governments. The Veterans Home of California is the largest of its kind in the nation and still maintains 750 acres of the original site.

After the state assumed control of the facility, it eventually replaced the frame structures with newer buildings. By 1932 a large hospital was constructed. During excavation for this project an unmarked grave was uncovered containing the remains of a man partially clad in a uniform dating back to the Indian wars. He became the Unknown Soldier of the Veterans Home of California.

The facility has been a source of pride for many groups in the Bay Area. Driving up the long driveway approaching the home, there is a row of elm trees on either side. These trees were donated to the home some years ago by San Francisco's Golden Gate Park; today the driveway is known as Avenue of the Elms.

The residents take pride in their home, which is a community unto itself. Many of the residents are actively employed in Napa Valley, giving them a sense of being productive. To be eligible for admission, a veteran must be a resident of California, must have served in the Armed Forces during wartime or in time of peace in a campaign or expedition, be aged or disabled, and have an honorable discharge.

There are many opportunities to be involved in the community whether it be in the form of employment, recreation, or an organization. One in-

The first hospital built in 1932 was named for Colonel Nelson Holderman (inset), commandant for twenty-eight years and Medal of Honor recipient. A new 56-bed, acute care addition to Holderman Hospital is under way.

volved group is The Historians. That organization recommended that the old Armistice Chapel be restored and then became involved in the restoration process. This picturesque little chapel was built on the grounds of the home about the time of the World War I armistice. Reconstruction was funded with state and federal grants and funds donated by home members and the City of Yountville.

One gentleman stated: "Before I came here my health was poor, and I was bent over with arthritis and could hardly walk. Now I eat well, my health has improved, and my arthritis is almost gone. I have found friends and a purpose in life. This is my home." That gentleman is more than ninety years old and as sharp and spry as someone many years younger.

Urban development as yet has not encroached into the community, and the area still has the feel of a rural setting, yet has the convenience of the small nearby community of Yountville. As a result, many of their services are interrelated and shared. The veterans can become registered voters as citizens of Yountville and are encouraged to run for public office.

The Veterans Home of California has become one of the major employers in Napa County. Many other individuals and groups volunteer their time and services. The same institution that was conceived by a private corporation is still fondly supported by the private community.

A.H. SMITH COMPANY

California has attracted pioneers from all walks of life and from all parts of the world. Not the least of these was Arthur H. Smith, founder of A.H. Smith Company, the oldest insurance agency in the Napa Valley.

As people moved westward and put down roots in California, they began to aquire property that needed to be insured. When Arthur H. Smith became an agent of Continental Insurance Company in 1890, little did he know that he was to become one of the first Continental agents to move to California.

As a child, Smith moved from England to the United States with his parents. The family settled in Marshfield, Missouri, where he was raised, met his wife, and began his family. From 1890 to 1897 Smith worked for Continental Insurance Company and achieved the position of state agent. In 1897 he came west with his family as the new state agent for Northern California. An indication that Smith was a pioneer in the insurance indus-

(Left to right) James Russell "Russ" Imrie, Sr., who retired at the age of eighty-six in 1974; H. Clyde Edmundson, vice-president of Continental Insurance Company; James R. Imrie, Jr., who retired in 1979; and Kenneth Imrie, still active today, gather for the presentation of a plaque to A.H. Smith Company on the 100th anniversary of Continental Insurance Company.

try was the size of his territory. He was assigned all of Northern California from San Francisco to the Oregon border and eastward to the Nevada state line.

In 1897 the family settled in Napa. One of Smith's daughters, Jessie, married James Russell "Russ" Imrie, Sr. This linked the Smith family to another pioneer family that had established roots in the Napa Valley in 1853.

William Imrie, a Scotsman, came to the United States with his parents as an infant. The family settled in New York State where he was raised. At the age of twenty-four, Imrie left New York to seek his fortune in the West, just as many others were doing at the time.

Imrie left New York by ship. After crossing the Isthmus of Panama, he boarded the S.S. *Independence*. As it steamed up the coast of Baja, the ship went aground near the island of Santa Margarita. During the captain's attempt to free the ship, the boilers blew up and the ship burned. In a panic, people were jumping off the ship on the landward side and perishing on the rocks below. Over 200 lives were lost. Seeing this, Imrie jumped into the water on the sea-

ward side and swam around the ship to the island. Marooned for two weeks, he and the other survivors were, at last, rescued by a whaler and brought to Sausalito. From there Imrie made his way to the gold fields and then on to Sutter's Fort where he became acquainted with a member of the Coombs family. When asked if he would come to Napa to work on Frank Coombs' ranch, Imrie readily accepted.

In 1860 he purchased 800 acres in the Silverado Trail-Hagen Road area, which was later referred to as Imrieville. In 1868 the acreage was sold, and Imrie purchased land on Big Ranch Road. The Imrie family still owns and occupies the property. Today Beringer Winery leases approximately ninety acres, which is planted in Chardonnay vines.

Imrie married Jane Nicoll and they raised seven sons and three daughters

Arthur H. Smith developed a good rapport with the Napa Fire Department and, on the occasion of the Smiths' fiftieth wedding anniversary, the firemen gathered while Chief Otterson presented a bouquet.

on the Big Ranch Road property. One of the boys, James Russell "Russ" Imrie, Sr., married Jessie Smith. In 1929 Russ joined the A.H. Smith Company. Since Arthur H. Smith's death in 1944, the Imrie family has carried on the family business.

Arthur H. Smith actively sold insurance for fifty-four years, from 1890 to 1944. He represented Continental Insurance Company, which is still the primary carrier for A.H. Smith Company. The early policies were written for fire insurance on farms, schoolhouses, and churches. With Continental's reputation for prompt claims settlement and Arthur H. Smith's authority as state agent, he was able to settle claims immediately. This was appreciated by farmers in the event of an agricultural fire. As soon as the fire moved beyond the insured's property, Smith wrote a draft and settled the claim on the spot.

"B-4-U-Burn-C-Smith" was his slogan, and it was retained for seventy-five years until the agency moved to the corner of Clay and Seminary in 1965. This slogan became popular as Smith traveled throughout Northern California by stagecoach, buggy, and, at times, horseback. He would be on the road for up to six months at a time. One humorous story recounts how, on a shorter trip, Smith traveled with the local haberdasher to share expenses. While the farmer they visited was being measured for a suit he was, at the same time, signing a fire insurance policy on his farmhouse and barn.

Initially, Smith maintained his office in his home. Later he moved to an office on the corner of Second and Main. In 1948 the firm's headquarters was moved to 1408 Second Street, where it remained until 1965. That year the agency moved into its new building and present site at the corner of Clay and Seminary.

(Inset) The original office at Second and Main with A.H. Smith and his two secretaries and the catchy "B-4-U-Burn" sign.

The present office at the corner of Clay and Seminary was built in 1965.

James R. Imrie, Sr., remained active in the business until his retirement in 1974 at the age of eighty-six. His sons, James Jr. and Kenneth, grandsons of Arthur H. Smith, joined the firm at the close of World War II after serving as line officers in the U.S. Naval Reserve. James Jr. joined the agency in 1946, and Kenneth followed three years later. Both are alumni of the University of California at Berkeley. Kenneth has served as state director of the Independent Insurance Agents and Brokers of California, and remains active in the business today. James Jr. retired in 1979.

Melvin Willback, CPCU (Chartered Property and Casualty Underwriter, the highest professional designation in the property and casualty insurance field), joined the agency in 1962. He is a graduate of the University of California at Berkeley and served as casualty manager for Continental Insurance Company before coming to A.H. Smith Company. He has also served as state director of the Independent Insurance Agents and Brokers of California. Charles

Niccolls associated his agency, the former William Ross Agency, with A.H. Smith Company in 1971. Niccolls is also a graduate of the University of California at Berkeley.

The business has continued to expand. Three great-grandsons of Arthur H. Smith have joined the nearly century-old agency. William, John, and Kent Imrie, all having the designation of CPCU, are graduates of the University of California at Davis, Santa Barbara, and Berkeley, respectively.

The firm's modus operandi has changed somewhat, but its tradition of service has not. Today computers help the office run more efficiently. Although soliciting clients is less rigorous than in the horse and buggy days, many policyholders have been retained throughout Northern California over a period of several generations. This speaks for the tradition of service offered by A.H. Smith Company.

Today A.H. Smith Company offers its clients a complete line of insurance products and services, both commercial and personal.

KAISER STEEL CORPORATION

Just as the Napa River has played an important role in the history of Napa County, the river has played an equally important role in the history of Kaiser Steel Corporation.

Basalt Rock Co., Inc., from whom Kaiser acquired its Napa plant, was founded September 15, 1924, by A.G. Streblow. Quarry operations began with Streblow manning the shovel and Edmond F. Brovelli handling the bookkeeping and stenographic work. The demand for the crushed stone grew and an aerial tramway was built from the quarry over the highway to the Napa River. The tramway was used to carry the rock to the river and dump it on wooden barges.

The Napa River provided access to Sacramento, Stockton, Oakland, San Francisco, and the entire West Coast. Basalt soon began to secure large contracts for riprap and jetty stone to be used for bank retention, but the wooden barges could not withstand the pounding of the large rock. In the late 1930s the firm began the design and construction of its own steel barges. The self-unloading barges had capacities of 750 and 1,000 tons each.

Skidways were laid along the east bank of the Napa River, and steel plate was purchased. The process of cutting and welding was begun, and soon Basalt was in the business of building barges.

In the late 1930s the United States began a preparedness program in re-

The launching ceremony of the first barge built by Kaiser since World War II. This barge was built and completely finished at the Napa facility.

sponse to the situation developing in Europe that ultimately led to World War II. Authorization was received by Basalt to build its first barge for the Navy in July 1940. Later the Navy awarded the firm additional contracts for barges.

When Australia entered the war, it contracted with Basalt for the con-

This aerial view of Kaiser Steel Corporation shows the pipe mill to the far right; the fabricating shop and machine shop is in the center. The river location makes it ideal for transporting large steel fabrications from the Napa plant.

struction of small ships. Later, upon the United States' entry into World War II, a complete shipyard, with a 1,000-foot concrete seawall and four dry docks, was built on Basalt property in Napa twelve miles above the Mare Island Navy yard. The Napa shipyard was constructed to accommodate the needs of the Navy for shipbuilding maintenance, reconversion, and dry docking for coastal vessels of all types. In February 1942 Basalt became one of the first local firms to receive the Navy "E" Award. Later it received the Army-Navy "E" Award in recognition of an outstanding production record.

The height of the shipbuilding period was from 1941 to 1944. In the postwar years Basalt began conversion to peacetime production. A plant to produce welded steel pipe was needed on the West Coast for the manufacture of line pipe for

transmitting water, petroleum, and gas. In 1948 Basalt made the decision to engage in steel pipe production in Napa.

The firm's engineers then began the task of designing the necessary machinery and equipment. The pipe mill equipment was completely manufactured in the company's own fabricating and machine shops. The pipe mill, known as an electric resistance weld (ERW) mill, had the capability of producing high-pressure steel pipe twelve to twenty inches in diameter

Due to permit restrictions preventing an underwater pipeline for transmitting oil from an offshore production platform to the shore, Exxon contracted with Kaiser Steel Corporation to build the single anchor leg mooring system. This project was entirely fabricated at Kaiser Steel's Napa facility.

and up to forty feet in length. Among the first pipe produced was for a thirty-mile water supply line from the Conn Dam into Napa.

In 1949 Basalt entered into a sales and manufacturing agreement with Kaiser Steel. Based on Kaiser Steel's capability to furnish the steel plate and market the pipe, in 1950-1951 Basalt built the first part of the large-diameter submerged arc-welded pipe mill at Napa. During that time the firm also became engaged in a general plate-fabricating operation.

In May 1955 an agreement was reached between Kaiser Steel and Basalt for Kaiser to purchase the plant site in Napa. When Kaiser Steel assumed ownership, the Napa facility was further expanded and upgraded. A large assembly bay was added to the plate shop in 1956. A second finishing line was added to the large-diameter pipe mill two years later, giving it the largest production capacity for pipe of that kind in the United States.

In 1962-1963 came a new forming line for the pipe mill, and in 1964 a second assembly bay was added to the plate shop. Two years later the original electric resistance weld (ERW) mill site was converted over to be used to build the subway liner rings for the Bay Area Rapid Transit System (BART).

In addition to the development of the physical plant, a highly skilled and capable staff has also been assembled. This combination of a premier facility and a skilled staff brought about steel fabrication that was unmatched west of the Mississippi. Recognition of the firm's achievements came when other steel companies began approaching Kaiser Steel to build pipe mills. The company went on to build and install pipe mill equipment in many nations of the world, including Japan, Germany, Great Britain, Canada, Brazil, Mexico, and Iran.

In addition, major fabricating contracts were acquired for offshore drilling rigs. In 1964 the first all-weather production platform was built for Cook Island, Alaska. That same year the firm constructed one of the first semi-submersible drilling rigs ever built. Kaiser Steel also completed fabrication work for a number of bridges in the western United States, including the San Mateo, Hayward, and the Dumbarton, the Pioneer Bridge in Sacramento, the Stockton Channel Bridge, and the New Me-

In the early days of Basalt-Kaiser, around 1950, a trainload of pipe is ready for delivery to the customer.

lones Reservoir Bridge. Several high-rise buildings were also fabricated and erected by Kaiser Steel, including the Transamerica Pyramid and Bank of America headquarters buildings in San Francisco and the Arco Towers in Los Angeles.

Basalt drew its work force from the local community. Many key employees began their careers with Basalt and later retired from Kaiser Steel Corporation. Some have never worked for another employer. Because the company was so diversified, employees could find a place where they could develop their natural abilities and skills. The firm also aided its employees in furthering their education and improving their vocational skills. This tradition was carried over to Kaiser Steel Corporation.

Examples of this policy are Ernest Ilsley, who began as a truck driver for Basalt in 1933 and retired as vice-president of Kaiser Steel's Fabricated Products Group in 1972, and James Maggetti, who was hired by Basalt as an estimator in 1948 and retired as vice-president of Kaiser Steel's Fabricated Products Group in 1983.

A.G. Streblow founded a company that has spanned six decades and now, as Kaiser Steel Corporation, has the capability as a leading manufacturer of fabricated steel products in the United States.

RAYMOND VINEYARD AND CELLAR

While the Raymond family is proud of its heritage, that of being descended from the Beringer family, the oldest wine-making family in the Napa Valley, it is even more proud of its new beginning in the wine-making industry. When explaining how family members planted the vineyard and built the first structures with their own hands, their pride is visible in their expressions.

The Beringer wine-making lineage can be traced to Jacob Beringer, who began producing wine for Charles Krug in 1870. The link between the Beringer family and the Raymond family is Roy Raymond, Sr. In 1933, shortly before the repeal of Prohibition, Roy Sr. began working for the Beringer winery. Two years later he married Martha Jane Beringer, Otto Beringer's daughter.

Roy Sr. worked his way up through the ranks of the business, becoming a wine maker and assistant general manager. When his sons, Roy Jr. and Walter, became old enough, they began developing an interest in agriculture and wine making. They later worked for their father on a part-time basis, doing whatever needed to be done and gaining practical experience in the wine-making industry. The brothers then went on to college to obtain the formal education necessary to prepare them to carry on in the wine-making industry.

Roy Jr. enrolled at U.C. Berkeley to study business education. He later was admitted to U.C. Davis for two years of viticulture and enology studies. Walter studied agricultural management at California Polytechnic State University. Following graduation the brothers returned to Beringer to put their education to practical use, Roy as vineyard manager and Walter as assistant wine maker. In 1970 it became necessary for the Beringer family to sell their winery, and Nestlé purchased the facility the following year. However, the Raymond family

Roy Jr., Roy Sr., and Walter Raymond are all actively involved in the day-to-day operation of Raymond Vineyard and Cellar.

had no difficulty in deciding their future. After a family conference the decision was made to purchase a good piece of land and start a small winery of their own.

After the sale of the Beringer winery, Roy Sr. stayed on for one year to help the new owners during the transition period. Roy Jr. remained for several more years to help with new planting. Walter, however, immediately began clearing the land that the family had purchased—ninety acres located off Zinfandel Lane.

Walking through the Raymond winery, the pungent aroma of grapes fermenting is both delightful and tantalizing. Everything is impeccably clean, and the state-of-the-art equipment is in place. Walking out into the vineyard, visitors step into a panorama of the Napa Valley. In the center of that panorama lies Raymond Vineyard and Cellar. The vineyard has been carefully planted, and the strong, healthy vines are a testi-

mony to those efforts.

When the Raymonds purchased the land, it consisted solely of walnut orchards. Walter's first task was to clear the land and prepare it for grapes. The first vines were planted in 1972 and 1973. By 1974 the family had harvested fifty tons of reds and had experienced their first crush.

The Raymonds have planted eighty of their ninety acres in vineyards. The other ten acres are utilized for home sites, the winery site, and frost ponds. In addition to caring for their own property, they also cultivate and manage 120 acres of vineyards for absentee owners.

Initially the family planted their land in eight varieties of grapes: Pinot Noir, Zinfandel, Napa Gamay, Johannisberg Riesling, Chenin Blanc, Merlot, Chardonnay, and Cabernet Sauvignon. At present, however, they

Roy Raymond, Jr., vineyard manager, driving the tractor on the ninety-acre vineyard that surrounds the winery.

Winemaker Walter Raymond draws a barrel sample from a tank in the family cellar.

are growing only Cabernet Sauvignon, Merlot, and Chardonnay. This represents an effort to limit the number of varieties of wines produced and to concentrate on quality.

The Raymonds' wine is estate grown and bottled, and having fewer varieties grown on-site allows the family a greater selection of grapes of each variety. The top 50 percent of the grapes can be used for their varietal wines, while the rest is suitable to be bottled under secondary labels or for bulk purposes. Since wine making begins with the grapes, it is an advantage to have fewer varieties to cultivate.

Roy Jr. and Walter work closely to produce the quality of wine desired beginning with the vineyard. "Basically we figure we grow wine," says Roy Sr. The Raymonds have the added advantage of the most modern, up-to-date facilities available for the production of their wine. Says

Walter, "The great technological leaps in wine making began in the early 1970s. We got in on the beginning of that period and were able to pioneer some of the changes ourselves."

The Raymonds' first bottle of wine was sold in 1977; 70,000 cases were sold in 1985. Their goal is 80,000 cases. Grape tonnage has jumped from 50 tons their first year in business to 1,550 tons in 1985.

The Raymonds' wine is marketed nationally through brokers, with 60 percent sold to restaurants. Half of the family's wine production is in Chardonnay, 20 percent is Cabernet Sauvignon, 10 percent is Fumé Blanc, and the balance is Chenin Blanc and Johannisberg Riesling.

The whole family has been involved in the development of the business. They planted their own vineyard and constructed the early buildings themselves. This spirit of cooperation is possible because they have a great deal of respect for each

other. Says Roy Sr., "We have always been a close family." It is obvious that he is proud of his sons, who are responsible for the management of Raymond Vineyard and Cellar. Roy Sr. once told his sons: "I have already served my apprenticeship." However, Walter states, "He works harder than any of us. He still takes a barrel apart and puts it back together."

The Raymond Vineyard and Cellar operation has grown from a pride in what the Raymonds do. "We can see it through from scratch to finish, beginning with the raw product," says Roy Sr. "Where else," adds Walter, "could we make a living and get as much enjoyment out of it?" The family tradition of wine making handed down over four generations appears to have maintained its momentum.

The Raymond family (from left): Roy Raymond, Jr., Walter Raymond, Martha Jane Beringer Raymond (seated), and Roy Raymond, Sr.

MARY LEE TILDEN MORTON
RUTHERFORD SQUARE

Sculptor, rancher, mother of four, Mary Lee Tilden Morton is a gourmet cook, designer-builder, innkeeper, and businesswoman.

Mary Tilden (her professional name) takes pride in her heritage as she speaks proudly of her grandfather, Major Charles Lee Tilden, a prominent figure in the early development of San Francisco. He was honored by having the East Bay's Tilden Park named after him. Of English descent, the ancestral family migrated to America in 1623—shortly after the Pilgrims landed at Plymouth Rock.

After receiving her B.A. in sculpture and also history of art at the University of California at Berkeley, Mary completed her training at the École des Beaux Arts in Geneva, Switzerland, obtaining her diplôme in 1951. Her bronze statues of Christ and Buddha are on the altar of the Temple of the Northern California Vedanta Society in San Francisco. In 1959 she won the first John Gregory Award (National Sculpture Society) for a Carrara marble classic female torso. Her many portraits and other bronzes are on display in public and private collections throughout the world.

In 1966 Mary took her four children to Switzerland to better their education by giving them a second language (French), as well as to take advantage of returning to her alma mater. Those three years resulted in scholastic improvement for her children and three sculpture exhibitions for Mary. One was a well-acclaimed, month-long show in Paris, another in Geneva, and the last in Hermance, Switzerland, where they were living.

Country life in the small town of Hermance appealed to Mary; and when she returned to America, she purchased a 124-acre ranch in Rutherford—in the heart of Napa Valley—and named it the "Merry M Ranch." Approximately half the

Mary Lee Tilden Morton and Tisha, one of her three dogs, sitting under the arched covered walkway overlooking the floral courtyard of her Rancho Caymus Inn.

property was planted in "choose and cut" Christmas trees; the balance was in grapes. Mary spent the first five years removing the trees and planting choice varietal vines. At the same time, this energetic lady spent two and a half years completely renovating the huge historical ranch house built in 1913 by a Napa Valley pioneer, Senator Seneca Ewer. She also found time to build her studio—a sculptor's dream.

With the completion of these projects, Mary embarked on her master project, which would occupy the next fourteen years: Rutherford Square. Purchasing several adjacent properties on the corner of Highway 29 and Rutherford Road, she designed and constructed, in 1973, the Beaulieu Wine Tasting Pavilion for the famous Beaulieu Winery. Next came "The Corner Bar," with its small kitchen named "Soup 'n Such" where Mary prepared all the soups and sandwiches herself. Accomplishments in 1975 included the Garden Restaurant and Rutherford Square Theatre. Rutherford Square's red-tiled roofs,

stone, stucco, and wrought-iron gates continue the historical feeling of the colonial Spanish style.

In May 1976 the Cottage Deli & Ice Cream was opened. A carefully renovated Victorian home built in 1896 was converted into a rustic restaurant decorated with period antiques and Moroccan rugs.

The masterpiece of Mary Tilden's fourteen-year dream, the Rancho Caymus Inn, was completed on May 20, 1985. Two years in design, three and a half in planning and construction, the facility stands on the land grant originally known as Caymus Rancho—a grant given to Napa Valley pioneer George Yount by the Mexican commandant of California, General Vallejo, more than 150 years ago. The inn, dedicated to the artists and craftsmen who created it, is compatible with the rest of Rutherford Square, as well as a reflection of its historical roots in Napa Valley.

While designing the inn, Mary found an eighty-year-old barn in Ohio that had beams and planking perfect for rustic construction. Persuading its owners to sell, she sent two Napa Valley master carpenters to dismantle the barn—an incredible job that took thirty-five days. They returned with more than 93,000 running feet of rare red and white oak, pine, cedar, and elm—some measuring over forty feet in length. A pole barn and shop were erected on the Merry M Ranch, in which the craftsmen created the inn's doors, stairs, railings, cabinet tops, and all the hand-hewn beams.

The cozy 26-room retreat is designed in a "U" shape around a central floral courtyard of winding hand-set paths of 100-year-old terra cotta roof tile. A unique stone fountain, a variety of indigenous plants and trees, and a colorful array of succulents greet the inn's guests during all seasons of the year. This private garden may be viewed from the arched balconies of the first level, or from the oak-railed balconies above. Each guest suite has its own private garden balcony overlooking the magnificent vineyards of central Napa Valley.

Each guest suite, unique in design and decor, is named for a prominent pioneer or settler who has left his or her imprint on Napa Valley. First-level suites have exposed hand-hewn ceiling beams; those on the second level have pitched beams, creating the cozy feeling of a cabin roof. All suites are split-level, with the lower

levels featuring unique beehive fireplaces (handmade by Mary when she was unable to get her idea across to her workmen). The combination of natural hewn wood, hand-thrown stoneware basins, and textured stucco walls emanates an earthy atmosphere. The master suites offer large jacuzzi tubs framed by stained glass windows, designed by a gifted local artist, and full kitchens to provide extra comfort for an extended visit.

Mary searched the highlands of Ecuador in her quest for beautiful woolen goods and "tapis" made by the Otavalon and Salazaca Indians. Hand dyed and handwoven, these colorful small rugs became bedspreads, pillow covers, and wall hangings. Rugs and carpets from Guana, a small town in Ecuador, complement the hardwood floors. Black walnut beds were designed and carved by

Above is the floral courtyard of Rancho Caymus Inn taken from the second-floor balcony. Below is the handset path of 100-year-old terra-cotta roof tile. The oak-railed balconies are made from an old barn built in Ohio in 1899.

the townspeople of St. Anton, Ecuador. The wrought-iron lamps especially created for the Rancho Caymus Inn came from Quito, capital of Ecuador, while the parota tables and chairs were hand-crafted in Guadalajara.

The inn's Caymus Kitchen will serve breakfast or lunch in the suites, balconies, central garden, or dining room; and the Mont St. John Room offers a comfortable, open-beamed room for weddings, receptions, meetings, and parties. The stained-glass windows, depicting aspects of Napa Valley, and a huge indoor-outdoor fieldstone fireplace add warmth and comfort to the rooms and private gardens.

Mary intends to return to work in her studio on her two-and-a-half-ton block of white Carrara marble she bought in Italy thirty years ago. Someday it will be an angel, designed to stand over the Tilden family plot at Mountain View Cemetery in Piedmont. Mary says, "I hope to have another twenty years to fulfill my real love—sculpture—so I may honor my Tilden family."

Mary Tilden's studio, a sculptor's dream of four rooms for different media, is built in a "U" shape overlooking the vineyards. The historical ranch house was built in 1913 by Napa Valley pioneer Senator Seneca Ewer.

TREFETHEN VINEYARDS

"Eshcol" is a Hebrew word meaning a cluster, especially of grapes, that is a biblical reference to the region of the land of Hebron where Moses' spies found the large clusters of luscious grapes.

The biblical name was also chosen by James and George Goodman, two prosperous bankers, for their 280-acre estate at the southern end of Napa Valley. The namesake vineyards, which similarly produced outstanding grapes, had been planted by California pioneer Joseph Osborne in 1856. Thirty years later the Goodmans' new winery, a wooden structure with a capacity of 250,000 gallons, was built in the heart of the parcel.

In 1888 the estate-bottled Eshcol Cabernet Sauvignon won first place at the San Francisco Viticultural Fair.

At the turn of the century the brothers retired and sold the property to J. Clark Fawver—a farmer who took pride in his vineyard. Fawver's death in 1940—leaving no direct descendants to care for the vineyard or produce wine, and preceded by

The old wooden winery was built in 1886 for James and George Goodman on their estate, Eshcol, by winery architect Captain Hamden McIntyre.

phylloxera, Prohibition, and the Depression—led to the closing and deterioration of the old wooden winery and the neglect of the vineyards.

In 1968 Gene and Katie Trefethen, forced from their previous ranch by urban development, acquired Eshcol and 320 adjoining acres. Tony Baldini came with them and brought with him his rare gift of communicating with nature and the soil. When Gene determined to rip out the old prune and walnut orchards and replant vines, the task was assigned to Tony. Under his direction every vine at Trefethen has been planted and meticulously cared for. As the fruit of Tony's labor began to come forth, the Trefethens' son, John, was put in charge of marketing the grapes. It was he who resolved that Trefethen Vineyards should enter the winemaking business, after making experimental lots of Chardonnay and Cabernet Sauvignon.

John developed a business plan for a small winery while attending Stanford Graduate School of Business. He began putting his plan into operation at Trefethen, and at the same time proceeded to remodel the old wooden winery building. In 1973, 2,000 cases of Chardonnay and Pinot Noir were produced. As growth took

place and John's responsibilities became greater, it became necessary to bring in an assistant. In 1975 David Whitehouse, Jr., a graduate of California at U.C. Davis, joined Trefethen as enologist. Under his guidance four premium varietal wines are produced: Chardonnay, Cabernet Sauvignon, White Riesling, and Pinot Noir. Two proprietary wines, a red and white, are labeled under the historic name of Eshcol. In 1985 the operation produced 60,000 cases of wine, all estate grown and bottled. Half of the grapes are retained for the winery's own production; the rest are sold to other Napa Valley wineries.

Janet Trefethen, John's wife, moved into the marketing position as John assumed the responsibilities of president and general manager. Her office is dominated by a large picture window, which frames the 600-acre vineyards and surrounding hills. Within the framework of that window, it could be Eshcol 1886 or Trefethen 1986—both denoting the "fertile valley."

John Trefethen, president and general manager of Trefethen Vineyards, with his wife, Janet, who is in charge of marketing.

HUNTINGTON BROS.

Dexter Huntington and one of the company trucks at the Covelo Road job in Mendocino County, 1959.

Hanging on the wall in Jim Huntington's office is a large site map of a $6-million project in Modesto: the wastewater storage ponds under contract for the City of Modesto. The levee work—being done by Huntington Bros.—will be extended over a period of two years, the first phase of which was completed in 1985.

This is quite a contrast from the early endeavors undertaken by the three Huntington brothers after they became partners and general contractors on February 13, 1948, in San Anselmo. They began with very basic equipment. Dexter had been in business for himself and brought in a 20B Bucyrus-Erie Dragline, a truck, trailer, and transport along with his business skills. Alfred "Fred" and Lucius brought in a North West Model 4 dragline and a Caterpillar Crawler Tractor, model #35. As time went on, new equipment was obtained under the partnership.

In the summer of 1948 the entrepreneurs moved their operation to Napa, where Dexter had property they could use. From an initial five-acre parcel, the property presently covers fifty-two acres adjacent to Silverado and Highway 121. The projects became larger also: In the beginning the brothers would contract and complete one project at a time, with each partner responsible for bidding and searching out work. In 1950 they gained recognition after doing the Washington Road project thirteen miles outside of Nevada City. From there they went to the coast to do highway work and grading; then came dams, levees, and irrigation wastewater storage. The brothers all operated the equipment and had little interest in administrative work. During these years their sons worked for them from time to time.

In 1963 Fred and Dexter purchased Lucius' share of the business. Fred's sons, Tom and Fred, were interested in the operation of heavy equipment and gained their skill and expertise by working in the field as operating engineers for various contractors and employers. Their field experience led to successful direct supervision of major highway and other earth-moving projects in California. Dexter's sons, Jim and Don, were more administrative-minded and went to college to obtain civil engineering degrees; Jim from the University of Nevada, and Don from San Jose State. One by one the young men began working for the company, and in 1968 all four bought into the business.

In 1972 the sons purchased controlling interest—with Tom and Fred acting as foremen and supervising the construction work, and Jim and Don handling the administrative work. One of the major jobs done in the Napa area by the second-generation Huntington Bros. was the Southern Crossing, for which it completed the road work and grading for the access roads to the main span. The firm, incorporated in 1983, is currently developing a vineyard in Wooden Valley as a satellite venture. During the summer season it carries as many as fifty employees on its payroll.

The philosophy handed down from the fathers that seems to make the family-business relationship work is this: Each person contributes what he does best. Fred and Dexter, now retired, still play an important role in the company as their sons refer to them for counsel.

Fred, Dexter, and Lucius Huntington in February 1959, as they were on the way to the bank to obtain their business loan. The first Huntington Bros. office is in the background.

SANDER, JACOBS, CASSAYRE AND GRIFFIN, INC.

Ernest Sander (standing) and Bernard R. Jacobs shortly after their partnership was established. Their first office was at 1322 Third Street in Napa. Photo circa 1947

There is no match for youth and enthusiasm. Two young entrepreneurs, Ernest Sander and Bernard R. Jacobs, found their niche after World War II and combined forces in 1947 to build a successful insurance business.

Both natives of Napa, they returned to the city after the war. Bernard R. "Jake" Jacobs, a first lieutenant in the Air Force, had flown thirty-one missions over Europe and Germany as a B-17 pilot. Ernest Sander served as an Army sergeant in the air training command.

Both had grown up, attended school, and established credibility in the community. With many friends in common, their lives became intertwined in the postwar period. While Jacobs was still trying to determine the direction of his life, his father, who was sales manager at Gasser Motors, suggested that he attend Golden Gate College with Charlie Niccolls, also a lifelong resident of Napa. Jacobs consented and he and Niccolls graduated from the insurance course, attaining their license to practice in the insurance field.

When approached by Jacobs as to a business partnership, Niccolls stated that he was happy at Gasser Motors and liked working in the accounting field. However, he suggested that Jacobs contact his brother-in-law, Ernie Sander, who had left his job at Basalt Rock Company to work as a solicitor for Jordan and Dennis, a real estate and insurance firm. Sander was receptive, and the pair began putting together a partnership. They were short on capital but long on enthusiasm.

They borrowed $4,000 from Bank of America through the G.I. Bill. When that ran out they almost gave up. However, Sander's parents came through and allowed the partners to borrow $2,500 against their house. This gave them the boost they needed to continue on until the business had become firmly established.

Their first office was at 1322 Third Street in Napa. They shared space with realtors Ned and Guy Hartman. Their twenty-five dollars per month rent included telephone answering services by the Hartmans' secretary. During the first two years they worked the business alone without the aid of clerical help, doing their own bookkeeping and typing.

Their marketing strategy was basic; Jacobs and Sander went out and knocked on doors. Otherwise known as "cold calling," they blocked the town off and called on virtually every home and business in the community, introducing themselves and selling insurance whenever they could. They worked ten hours a day, six days a week, building their reputation and their business. They would have monthly sales contests with each other, with a twenty-five dollar bonus

for the winner.

In those days insurance was less sophisticated and people carried minimal amounts of coverage, usually only enough fire insurance on their homes to satisfy the requirements of the bank. Seldom were personal belongings or automobiles covered. As a result, Jacobs and Sander dealt almost exclusively with personal lines. Home owners were encouraged to upgrade their coverage to match the current market value of their home and were advised to cover the contents and their personal belongings.

Two years after starting the business Jacobs and Sander moved their office into the Lovejoy Mansion at 1516 Third Street. They later purchased the building. By 1957 the pair had constructed their own office building at 1810 Jefferson Street, which gave them 800 square feet of space. They had a clerical staff of two, allowing Jacobs and Sander to spend more time in the field.

At the same time the needs of the marketplace became more sophisticated, as did insurance coverage. In order to keep up with the changes, the partners upgraded their skills by taking more advanced courses of instruction, becoming better equipped to write commerical lines insurance. Later Jacobs began taking courses in preparation for attaining the professional designation of chartered Property and Casualty Underwriter (CPCU). He received that designation in 1969.

Bruce Cassayre, who served in the U.S. Army during the Korean War, joined the firm in 1959 with a degree in accounting from the University of San Francisco.

Glenn Griffin joined the company with twenty years of underwriting and management experience. He served with the 106th Infantry Division in Europe and was held prisoner for five months. Griffin took over the administrative duties of the firm.

Jacobs' son, Stephen, joined the firm in 1978, bringing with him four years' experience as an underwriter with an insurance company and three years' experience as a commercial account executive with a large insurance brokerage firm. Stephen has a degree in economics from California State University, Sacramento, and has completed four years of study toward the Chartered Property and Casualty Underwriter designation. He also served in the 4th Infantry Division in the Vietnam War. In addition, Jacobs' daughter, Susan, is responsible for group life and health benefit programs.

Bill Eagleton joined Sander, Jacobs, Cassayre and Griffin, Inc., in 1979 after taking early retirement from Industrial Indemnity in San Francisco. He was graduated from Colorado College and served in the U.S. Marine Corps in the South Pacific during World War II.

In 1983 Steven Reinbolt joined the firm, moving from Orange County, California, where he had served as a large-lines underwriter with the Insurance Company of North America. He graduated from the University of California at Santa Barbara with a bachelor's degree in economics and received his master's degree in business from the American Graduate School of International Management.

In 1979 a large office structure was built for the firm at 1810 Jefferson Street, more than tripling its space to 2,700 square feet. Today the company is one of the largest in Northern California with gross sales in excess of seven million dollars. Currently, there is a staff of sixteen well-trained, dedicated employees who now participate in a profit-sharing program.

Sander, Jacobs, Cassayre and Griffin, Inc., serves Napa, Solano, and Sonoma counties. It is able to offer a well-rounded program of coverages, enabling agents to assist clients in planning a complete package of insurance.

Ernest Sander retired at age sixty-five after nearly forty years of dedicated service to the agency.

"Jake" Jacobs remains active and as enthusiastic today as he was in the beginning. He states, "The early years were exciting but nothing like today. I could retire, but I'm having too much fun. The business is really dynamic and changing. We have these young guys coming in with a lot of great ideas and it's a lot of fun. Now is really the best time."

The current staff of Sander, Jacobs, Cassayre and Griffin, Inc.

CENTRAL VALLEY BUILDERS SUPPLY

Robert E. "Pat" Patterson gained knowledge and expertise in business principles from his father. This background, coupled with his own sales, marketing, and management skills acquired from working in the food-manufacturing industry, laid the groundwork for him to own and operate his own business. After a good deal of traveling and many moves Patterson and his wife, the former Eveleth Clark, decided to go into business for themselves in a desireable area where they could settle and put down roots.

In 1955 the ideal opportunity presented itself. Central Valley Builders Supply in St. Helena was for sale. It was a small town setting yet with easy access to major suppliers in San Francisco. It also had built-in roots. Eleveth's grandparents, the John Moodys, had moved to St. Helena from Fresno in the 1890s. Eveleth's mother, Helen Moody Clark, was raised in St. Helena, and after the death of her husband, returned to the city and reestablished residence there.

The conditions and setting were desirable and in September 1955 Patterson purchased Central Valley

Central Valley Builders Supply's new store in St. Helena. Built in 1979 on four acres, it has one acre under roof.

Builders Supply from Frank Creasy, who had established the business with Alexander Hamilton in March 1953.

When Patterson assumed ownership there were three employees and an inventory of $35,000, consisting of lumber, building supplies, and some hardware. The company's equipment included one forklift, one truck, and a pickup. The firm operated out of approximately 1,000 square feet of retail space.

In the beginning the Pattersons worked long hours—Pat building the business and Eveleth keeping books. They later expanded the business and became an integral part of the community by applying that "Extra Effort," their firm's motto.

The couple believes that their employees are their greatest asset, and an extra effort is made to treat them fairly and honestly and compensate them with a fair wage. And, as a result, the employees respond when called upon.

During the 1986 flood, employees worked day and night cleaning up the flood-damaged Napa store. It was operational within a few days. Later a steak dinner was held in the warehouse in appreciation for the team effort.

Central Valley Lumber has become incorporated with Robert E. Patterson, Sr., as chairman of the board, Robert E. Patterson, Jr., as president and general manager, Michael D. Micheli as vice-president, Robert Jessell as assistant general manager, Eveleth Patterson as treasurer, and Kathleen Patterson as secretary.

By 1979 the company had outgrown its original site. A new store was built on a four-acre site on Vintage Avenue in St. Helena with one acre under roof. In 1983 a second store was erected in Napa. When it was 90-percent framed, a windstorm blew it down. Later it survived the flood of 1986.

Both the Patterson family and Central Valley Builders Supply have deep roots in Napa Valley. The business is productive, with all revenues going back to Napa County. Each store employs between forty-five and fifty people, thus creating more jobs for the community.

Sixteen-year-old Stephen C. Patterson is becoming involved in the company, and his brother Robert Adam is not far behind. They represent the third generation of the Patterson family to be involved in the business and the fifth generation of the Napa Valley pioneer family. The Pattersons have built a legacy that will serve the community for years to come.

An aerial view of Central Valley Builders Supply's original site in St. Helena as it appeared when it was purchased in 1955.

FAMILY DRUG

Born of Italian immigrant parents, Mary Ann Doud—owner of Family Drug—attributes much of her success to the initiative and stalwartness passed on to her by her parents.

Her father, Sante Durlo, arrived in San Francisco in 1906 from Verona, Italy. Her mother, Cecilia Bombonato, followed in 1913.

From left to right: Ruth Brandlin, Barbara Soltis, pharmacist Thomas E. Gracia, Vickie Altamura, and Gaylon Kastner have been with Family Drug from ten to twenty-seven years.

Mary was born and raised in San Francisco. It was there as a child she played hours on end with an old scale from her uncle's store. Her sandbox became a store and there she filled and weighted bottles and pillboxes, an early indication of the direction her life was going to take. Mary's parents did not try to influence her regarding her career. They did, however, emphasize that she should take full advantage of her talents.

She worked for a dentist from the age of twelve, translating for his Italian patients on Saturdays. Mary continued to work for him through her high school and business college years, and he encouraged her to become a dental hygienist. Her interest in pharmacy could not be stifled, however, and on the day she was to begin dental hygienist school she passed the facility and continued on the streetcar to Parnasus Avenue. It was there at the University of Cali-

fornia Pharmacy College that she got off and walked in, handed them her credentials, and said she wanted to attend pharmacy school. She was accepted and became one of only six women to graduate in her class.

Not yet old enough to practice pharmacy, she continued working part time for Ramsey's Pharmacy in San Francisco to retain her touch. Mary also worked part time for I. Magnin and it was there that she began developing her interest in cosmetics and perfumes.

Napa Valley was a familiar place to Mary during her youth and college days. As a child she made many trips to the area with her family. They came by boat from the city and at Vallejo transferred to the Napa Electric Railway train and continued on to Yountville. Her father was an expert grafter of vines and would work in the vineyards on weekends while Mary and her mother spent time at Stags Leap Manor.

When a pharmacy located on Brown Street in Napa became available, it was only natural that Mary decided to purchase it and move there. In just two short years she decided to open a second store at the newly refurbished Food City Shopping Center. She moved into her present location at 1825 Old Sonoma Road on November 2, 1952, and named it Family Drug. Mary began with three employees, plus herself as the pharmacist. She closed the Brown Street store in 1954 and devoted her time to developing Family Drug into a reputable pharmacy with the largest supply of prescription drugs in Napa. Over the years she has expanded three times and now has ten employees and a second pharmacist, Thomas E. Gracia, who has been part of Family Drug for ten years.

Mary Doud is community minded and tries to help young people who are seeking work experience. Since

Mary Doud, pharmacist and owner of Family Drug, as she prepares prescriptions in her pharmacy.

opening Family Drug she has hired many high school students as delivery drivers in order to expose them to the field of pharmacy. While president of the Napa County Pharmaceutical Association, she initiated two scholarships for the study of pharmacy: one each for a junior college student and a high school student.

Mary was a member and director of the former Northern California Pharmaceutical Association and in 1965 was selected by that organization as Pharmacist of the Month. Mary is also a member of the National Association of Retail Druggists, the California Pharmaceutical Association, and the local Napa Valley Pharmacy Association. She is also a life member of the Napa County Historical Society in which she and her husband, executive director Jess Doud, actively participate.

INGLENOOK-NAPA VALLEY

This artist's rendering depicts the Inglenook Vineyard property in Napa Valley.

Inglenook Vineyard, established by retired sea captain Gustave Niebaum in 1879, has come full circle back to its warm and cozy nook nestled among the wooded foothills of Rutherford. The founder purchased three parcels of land, located on a portion of Caymus Rancho, extending from Rutherford west to the foothills. A previous owner had named one of the parcels Inglenook, which is a Scottish architectural term meaning "a warm and cozy corner." This designation so appealed to Captian Niebaum that he retained it.

The entrepreneur was born in Helsingfors, Finland, in 1842, and obtained his master's papers at age nineteen. On his first command, in 1864, he sailed to Alaska—where he gained the respect of the traders—and when the United States purchased that country three years later, he sailed to San Francisco with his cargo of furs. Renewing his acquaintance with many of the traders led to his becoming one of the founders of the Alaska Commercial Company, incorporated in 1869, which subsequently played a considerable part in the growth of the Alaskan territory.

On his many trips to Europe for the firm, Niebaum developed an enthusiasm for fine wines and their production. Two of his business associates—General John F. Miller, Civil War veteran, and Tiburcio Parrott—encouraged him to look for property in Napa Valley, an area that seemed to be the ideal location to further pursue his hobby by establishing a vineyard and winery.

Niebaum's ability to speak five languages and read several more enabled him to peruse foreign publications and books on the production of

Gustave Niebaum founded the winery in 1879.

grapes and fine wines. He amassed a vast library, from all over the world, which today is the most extensive library of pre-1900 books on the subject of viticulture and enology in existence. This collection is housed at the Inglenook Museum and the University of California at Davis.

With the immense fortune amassed from his founding the Alaskan Commercial Company, Niebaum was able to indulge in his labor of love. After purchasing his property in 1879, he began his step-by-step program to develop the great vineyards and winery he had envisioned. First he began experimenting with the facilities and grape varieties on hand. As he traveled to Europe he collected soil samples and vine cuttings from the finest vineyards, as well as vast information on the climate of each region's growing season. Additionally, he studied the cultural methods of the European vineyards. The Inglenook vineyards were greatly influenced by the most modern techniques then used in Bordeaux.

Greatly influenced by the studies of Louis Pasteur, Niebaum can be credited for being the first to bring science to Napa Valley wine making. He also was the first to adopt the trend, then starting in Bordeaux, to sell his wine exclusively in glass and to warrant the purity of every bottle sold.

The winegrower was untiring in his perfectionist efforts—using the best grapes that he was able to produce in an exceptionally constructed plant, with every phase of the operation scrupulously clean. His efforts were fruitful: His wines first gained recognition in international competition in the Paris exposition of 1889, and continued to take prizes throughout his lifetime. Inglenook's prize-winning wine of the period was Black Label

Claret-The Medoc Blend. The great Niebaum diamond logo was developed in the 1880s and is the only symbol of its kind to be utilized over 100 years.

After its founder's death in 1908, Inglenook Vineyard was successively under the direction of members of the second and third generations of the family—each striving to maintain the quality and distinction suggested by the name Inglenook and Gustave Niebaum.

John Daniel, Jr., great-nephew of Captain Niebaum, joined the operation in 1934 after graduating from Stanford University as a civil engineer. As the family had never considered its vineyards a source of income, it was able to maintain them throughout Prohibition. As the restraining laws ended, Inglenook petitioned the government to allow the great 1933 vintage to be accepted as legally saleable. The winery's Cabernet Sauvignon that year became famous both for its great quality and as a symbol of the end of a destructive era in American history.

Daniel had a remarkable ability to bring outstanding people to Inglenook, and to manage creative and

The original vine-covered winery built by Gustave Niebaum has been restored and is now being used as the Inglenook Museum.

difficult personalities. He insisted that quality and prestige remain the priority. However, family health problems and lack of capital to replant, update, and expand the winery forced him in 1963 to sell it to Louis Petri—owner of Allied United Vintners, Inc.

Subsequently, Inglenook became buried in the corporate world, and quickly became a wine operation that neither Daniel nor Niebaum would have recognized. In 1969 Hueblein purchased United Vintners from Allied, and its priority to expand the mass-marketed wines meant continued neglect of specialty wines such as the Napa Valley wines of Inglenook.

By the mid-1970s Hueblein began to focus on Inglenook Vineyards, and the circle began to close. The winery's centennial year was approaching—reason enough to renew the historic charm of the picturesque old stone structure and vineyard nestled in its "cozy corner."

Entering the wine museum is like a trip back in time. Housed there is part of the captain's library of books

on wines and vines and the brass die used for the great Niebaum logo—and once again used for today's diamond logo—which graces a new line of reserve wines introduced in 1985. In the wine library one will find wines dating back to 1882 that rivaled the finest in the world. With the replanting of the vineyards during the 1970s, there was great effort to maintain the original Niebaum clones, which were the primary historical source of Cabernet Sauvignon (as well as Merlot, Cabernet Franc, and Pinot Noir) in Napa Valley.

Finally, the circle was completed: Inglenook-Napa Valley was established and granted full autonomy in January 1983; and a strong and enthusiastic management team, with Dennis Fife as vice-president and general manager, was placed on-site. Fife relates, "We again have great grapes, great wine-making facilities, and great people; and we are back to the single focus of making great wines. Inglenook-Napa Valley is again carrying on the great traditions initiated by Captain Niebaum and carried on by John Daniel, Jr."

A recent advertising promotion reflects a renewed commitment to Inglenook's century-old tradition of wine-making excellence.

PATRONS

The following individuals, companies, and organizations have made a valuable commitment to the quality of this publication. Windsor Publications and the Napa County Historical Society gratefully acknowledge their participation in *Napa Valley: From Golden Fields to Purple Harvest.*

Barwick-Duttons Stationery and Office
   Products*
Bell Products, Inc.*
Beringer Vineyards
Blackney and Marsh Floors
Bookends Book Store
Mr. and Mrs. Arthur P. Carroll
Central Valley Builders Supply
Chaudhary & Associates, Inc.
   Engineers/Surveyors/Planners
Stanley E. Cliff
Crown Realty*
The Balthasar Darms Family
Rene and Veronica di Rosa
Jess Doud
Family Drug*
Franciscan Vineyards
The Gallery on Main Street
The Gaudino Family
Greene's Napa Cleaners
Halliday Bookstore
J.E. Heitz
Huntington Bros.*
Hurd Beeswax Candles
Inglenook-Napa Valley*
Kaiser Steel Corporation*
Hanns Kornell Champagne Cellars*
KVON/KVYN Radio*
Mr. and Mrs. Ronald L. Losel
Joseph Mathews Winery
Joel Momsen, C.P.A.
Robert Mondavi Winery
Mary Lee Tilden Morton
   Rutherford Square*
Napa City-County Library
Napa County Farm Supply

Stella Williams, Mgr.
Napa Land Title Company
Napa State Hospital*
Napa Valley Bank*
Napa Valley Lodge*
Napa Valley Natural History Association
Pacific Union College*
Queen of the Valley Hospital*
Raymond Vineyard and Cellar*
Roberts Bel Aire
St. Helena Hospital and Health Center*
Sander, Jacobs, Cassayre and Griffin, Inc.*
V. Sattui Winery
Sawyer of Napa
Silverado Country Club and Resort*
Slinsen Construction Company*
A.H. Smith Company*
Stag's Leap Wine Cellars
Sutter Home Winery
Trefethen Vineyards*
Vanderbilt and Co.
Veterans Home of California*
Villa Mt. Eden Winery
Westberg Mfg. Inc.
White Sulphur Springs

*Partners in Progress of *Napa Valley: From Golden Fields to Purple Harvest.* The histories of these companies and organizations appear in Chapter 7, beginning on page 113.

BIBLIOGRAPHY

BOOKS & MANUSCRIPTS

Archuleta, Kay. *The Brannan Saga.* San Jose: Self-published, 1977.

Bancroft, Hubert Howe. *History of California.* San Francisco: The History Company, 1886.

Bartlett, John Russell. *Personal Narratives of Explorations and Incidents in Texas, New Mexico, California, Sonora, and Chihuahua.* 2 Vols. New York: Appleton, 1854.

Beck, Warren A., and Ynez D. Haase. *Historic Atlas of California.* Norman, OK.: University of Oklahoma Press, 1974.

Bowles, Samuel. *Our New West.* Chicago: Hartford, 1869.

Brewer, William H. *Up and Down California in 1860-64.* New Haven: Yale University Press, 1930.

Calistoga Centennial, 1959. Napa: D. Crawford Assoc., 1959.

Camp, Charles, Ed. *James Clyman; American Frontiers Man, 1792-1881.* San Francisco: California Historical Society, 1928.

City of Napa. *Charter and Ordinances of the City of Napa.* Napa: City of Napa, 1884.

Cook, Sherburne F. *The Conflict Between the California Indian and White Civilization.* Berkley: University of California Press, 1976.

Drury, Aubrey. *California: An Intimate Guide.* New York: Harper & Co., 1947.

Dutton, Joan Parry. *They Left Their Mark.* St. Helena, CA.: Self-published, 1983.

Gregory, Thomas Jefferson. *History of Solano and Napa Counties.* Los Angeles: Historic Record Co., 1912.

Handbook of Calistoga Springs or Little Geysers. San Francisco: Alta California Book Co., 1897.

Hanrahan, Virginia. *Historical Napa Valley.* Series of articles which appeared in the *Napa Register* Centennial edition, 1948.

Heizer, R.F., and M.A. Whipple. *The California Indians.* Berkeley: University of California Press, 1951.

Hendricks, Gordon. *Eadweard Muybridge: The Father of the Motion Picture.* New York: Grossman Publisher, 1975.

Hoffman, Ogden. *Reports of Land Cases Determined in the U.S. District Court for the Northern District of California June Term 1853 to June Term 1858.* San Francisco: Hubert, 1862.

Hunt, Marguerite, and Harry Lawrence Gunn. *History of Solano County and Napa County.* Chicago: S.J. Clarke Publishing, 1926.

Illustrations of Napa County, Cal. Fresno: Valley Publishers, 1974. Facsimile of 1878 Smith and Elliott edition.

Issler, Anne Rolle. *Stevenson at Silverado.* Fresno: Valley Publishers, 1974.

Jones, Idwal. *Vines in the Sun.* New York: Morrow and Co., 1949.

Kernberger, David and Kathleen. *Mark Strong's Napa Valley, 1886-1924.* St. Helena: Historic Photos, 1978.

Ketteringham, William James. "The Settlement Geography of Napa Valley." Unpublished dissertation, Stanford, 1961.

King, Norton L. *Napa County: An Historical Overview.* Napa: Napa County Superintendent of Schools, 1967.

Kingsbury, Ralph. "The Napa Valley to 1850." Unpublished dissertation, USC, 1939.

Kroeber, A.L. *Handbook of the Indians of California.* New York: Dover Publications, 1976.

Marinacci, Barbara, and Rudy Marinacci. *California's Spanish Place-Names: What They Are and How They Got Here.* San Rafael: Presidio Press, 1980.

Napa City and County Portfolio and Directory. Napa: H.A. Darms, c. 1908.

Palmer, Lyman L. *History of Napa and Lake Counties, California.* San Francisco: Slocum, Bowen and Co., 1881.

Revere, Joseph Warren. *Naval Duty in California.* Oakland: Biobooks, 1974.

Saul, S. *Souvenir Advertisement of Napa County, CA.* Napa: Napa County Souvenir Co., 1901.

Stevenson, Robert Louis. *Silverado Squatters.* New York: Charles Scribner, 1897.

_____. *Treasure Island.* New York: Grosset and Dunlap, 1947.

Swasey, William F. *The Early Days and Men of California.* Oakland: Pacific, 1891.

Swett, Ira L., and Harry C. Aitken, Jr. *The Napa Valley Route.* Glendale, CA.: Self-published, 1975.

Thorton, S. Quinn. *Oregon and California in 1848.* New York: Harper, 1949.

U.S. Works Progress Administration, Federal Writer's Project. *California: A Guide to the Golden State.* New York: Government Printing Office, 1939.

U.S. Works Progress Administration, Northern California Historic Records Survey. *Inventory of the County Archives of California, No. 29, Napa Valley.* San Francisco: Government Printing Office, 1941.

Utt, Walter C. *A Mountain; A Pickax; A College.* Angwin, CA.: Pacific Union College, 1968.

Verardo, Denzil, and Jennie Dennis Verardo. *The Bale Grist Mill.* Oakland: California State Parks Foundation, 1984.

_____. *In the Valley of Bottled Poetry.* Pacific Grove, CA.: Boxwood Press, 1983.

Wallace, W.F., Ed. *History of Napa County.* Oakland: Enquirer Print, 1901.

Wood, Ellen Lamont. *George Yount;*

The Kindly Host of Caymus Rancho. San Francisco: Grabhorn Press, 1941.

Wright, Elizabeth Cyrus. *The Early Upper Napa Valley.* Stanislaus, CA.: California State College, 1974. Reprint from 1928.

Wright, Ralph B., Ed. *California's Missions.* Arroyo Grande, CA.: Hubert Lowman, 1976.

PERIODICALS

Avery, Constance. "Spa-ing in California." *Western Collector,* August, 1966, pg. 5.

Camp, Charles L. "William Alexander Trubody and the Overland Pioneers of 1847." *California Historical Quarterly,* XVI (June, 1937), 122-134.

Coyle, Charles W. "Life in an Insane Asylum." *Overland Monthly,* Vol. 21, 1893.

Davis, Fenelon. "Mines and Mineral Resources of Napa County, CA." *California Journal of Mines and Geology,* XLIV (April, 1948), 158-188.

"Frontier Journal of Sir James Douglas: A Voyage From the Columbia to California in 1840." *California Historical Quarterly,* VIII (June, 1928), 100-110.

Grieg, Jack R. "The Vessels of the Napa River, 1844-1890." *Gleanings,* III (February, 1984), No. 4.

Lyman, W.W. "The Lyman Family." *Gleanings,* II (April, 1980), No. 4.

Royers, Fred B. "Bear Flag Lieutenant: The Life Story of Henry L. Ford (1822-1860)." *California Historical Quarterly,* XXIX (September, 1950), 261-278.

Tortorolo, Mario J. "History of the City of Napa Water Supply." *Gleanings,* II (May, 1978), No. 2.

Verardo, Jennie, and Denzil Verardo. "Dr. Edward Turner Bale and His Grist Mill." *Gleanings,* II (June, 1979), No. 3.

Wichels, John. "A Brief Biological Sketch of Charles Hopper." *Sketches,* 1979.

_____. "Centennial Anniversary of Rutherford, 1876-1976." *Sketches,* 1979.

_____. "John Lawley: Pioneer Entrepreneur." *Gleanings,* III (February, 1982), No. 1.

_____. "The Pioneer One-Room Schools of Napa County." *Sketches,* 1979.

NEWSPAPERS
Napa Journal
Napa Register
Napa Reporter
Sacramento Bee
St. Helena Star
San Francisco Call
San Francisco Chronicle
Weekly Calistogan

INDEX

PARTNERS IN PROGRESS INDEX

Barwick-Duttons Stationery and Office Products, 116-117
Bell Products, Inc., 125
Central Valley Lumber, 152
Crown Realty, 124
Family Drug, 153
Huntington Bros., 149
Inglenook-Napa Valley, 154-155
Kaiser Steel Corporation, 142-143
Kornell Champagne Cellars, Hanns, 128-129
KVON/KVYN Radio, 134
Morton, Mary Lee Tilden Rutherford Square, 146-147
Napa County Historical Society, 114
Napa State Hospital, 136-137
Napa Valley Bank, 122-123
Napa Valley Lodge, 126-127
Pacific Union College, 118-119
Queen of the Valley Hospital
Raymond Vineyard and Cellar, 144-145
St. Helena Hospital and Health Center, 120-121
Sander, Jacobs, Cassayre and Griffin, Inc., 150-151
Silverado Country Club and Resort, 115
Slinsen Construction Company, 135
Smith Company, A.H., 140-141
Trefethen Vineyards, 148
Veterans Home of California, 138-139

GENERAL INDEX
Italicized numbers indicate illustrations.

Aetna Mine, 80
Aetna Springs Resort, 91
African Methodist Church, 70
Agriculture, 42-43, 45, 54, *105, 106. See also* Wine industry
Air pollution, 103
Altimura, José, 8, 12, 16
Amelia (ship), 39
Angwin, 20, 67, 96
Anti-Chinese Leagues, 87
Arcata, 69
Armory, 94, 95

Badham, Alexander, 80
Bailey, A.J., 79
Bain, Thomas, 82
Bale, Caroline, 48
Bale, Edward Turner, 8, 20-23, 25, 33, 48, 104
Bale, Maria Ignacia Soberanes, 20
Bale, Maria Ignacia Soberanes, 7, 8, 9, *21,* 22, 24, 28, 29, 30, 43, 65, 104; operators of, *22*
Bale Grist Mill State Historic Park, 23, 104
Ballooning, Hot-air, *112*
Barnes, Sara, 106; *Towards Diamond Mountain, 107*
Barnett, Elias, 28
Bartlett, John Russell, 25, 39
Basalt Rock Company, 97, 98
Bay area, 103
Bear Flag Rebellion, 8, 17, 25, 28, 29
Bear Flag Republic, 28
Beaulieu Winery, 52
Benecia, 9, 34, 40
Beringer, Charles, *48*
Beringer, Frederick, 9, *48,* 49, 50
Beringer, Jacob, 9, *48,* 49
Beringer Brothers, *48,* 49-50

Beringer Brothers wine cellar and residence, 9, *48,* 49, 50, 58, 85
Berryessa, José, 20
Berryessa, Ygnacio, 20
Berryessa Valley, 9, 20, 33, 34, 99
Bidwell-Bartleson Party, 24
Boardinghouses, 84
Boles, Charles, 37
Bothe-Napa Valley State Park, 69
Bourne, William, 55
Brannan, Sam, 8, 33, 80, *87,* 88-90, 103, 104
Bridger, Jim, 25
Brown, J.E., 30
Buckman, O.H., 4

California Pacific Railroad Company, 90
California Steam Navigation Company, 39
California Veteran's Home, 9, 73
California Water Project, 9, 99
California Wesleyan College, 69
California Wine Association, 55, 56, 57-58
Calistoga, 8, 9, 10, 12, 13, 20, 29, 33, 37, 39, 40, 41, 51, 64, 65, 66, 69, 70, 71, 75, 77, 79, 80, 85, 89, 90, 91, 99, 103, 104, *105*
Calistoga Depot, *38,* 39
Calistoga Free Public Library, 9, 68; children's corner of, *68*
Calistoga Hotel, 37, 89
Calistoga Methodist Church, 70
Calistoga Mineral Water Company, 9, 91
Calistoga Mining Company, 80
Calistogan, 9, 74
Calistoga Soaring Center, 9, 111
Calistoga Sparkling Mineral Water, 91
Calistoga Springs Resort, 87, *88, 89,* 90
Calistoga Township, 63
Callizo, Joseph, 54

Callustro Company, 104
Calnap, 82
Cameron Shirt Factory, 83
Carpy, Charles, 55-56
Carpy family, 59
Carquinez Bridge, 84
Carson, Kit, 8
Casey, James, 63
Castro, Francisco, 8, 16
Catholic Church (first), 8, 71
Catholics, 69, 70
Cattle raising, 22, 23, 30
Central School, 9, *64,* 66
Charles III, 15
Chiles, Joseph B., 8, 20, 24
Chiles Valley, 24
Chinese Exclusion Act, 87
Chinese population, 84-87
Christian Brothers, 7, 9, 55, 58, 59, 67; winery of, 58, *59* 103
Cinnabar, 8, 13, 79, 80
Cities and Towns. *See* individual cities and towns
Civilian Conservation Corps, 96
Clark, Abraham, 33; ranch of, *33*
Clark and Company, A.G., 74
Climate, Napa Valley, 13
Clothing industry, 83
Clyman, Hannah, 25
Clyman, James, 8, 9, 18, 24-25, 28, 29; residence and farm of, *24*
Clyman-McMahon party, 29
Coit, Lillie Hitchcock, *86*
Coloma, 29, 46
Columbia River, 18
Commercial Wireless and Development Company, 76, 77

Communication, 40-41
Conn Dam, 9, 83, 99
Contra Costa County, 40, 90
Coombs, Frank, 94
Coombs, Nathan, 8, 28, 30, 37, 71
County Board of Supervisors, 9, 103
Courthouses: (1856), 31, 69; (1878), 31, 62, 94, 95
Court House Square, 94
Crane, George B., 48
Crime, 63, 65, 75-76
Crystal Geyser Water Company, 91
Cyrus, J., 79

Daily Advertiser, 74
Daniel, John, Jr., 59
Davies, Jack, 59
De La Salle Institute, 67
Depression, Great, 58, 95-97
Dolphin (steamboat), 8, 37
Donner Party, 8, 28-29, 42, 65, 104
Doud, Jess, 7
Droughts: (1863-1865), 8; (1976-1977), 9, 99

Earthquake of 1906, 57-58
Education, 60, 64, 65-67.
Elections, Napa County, 30
Embarcadero, 30, 37
Empire Saloon, 31
English, Buck, 37
Escondido, 90
Evans, Charles, 91
Ewer, Seneca, 52
Ewer Winery, F.S., *52-53*
Excelsior Brass Band, *92*

"Falcon Crest," 54
Federal Writer's Project, 97
Ferrogiaro, Louis, 83
Ferro Glove Company, 83
Fire protection, 86
First Presbyterian Church, 9, 71
Fling, Guy, 8, 18
Flood of 1986, 9, *100-102*
Fort Lewis, 95
Fort Ross, 12, *14,* 15, 16, 46, 71
Fosdick, Sarah Graves, 8, 29, 65
Foss, Clark, 37
Francis Hospital, 73
Freemark Abbey, 59
Freeze, Andy, *95*
Frémont, John C., 8, 27, 28
Frisbie, John, 31
Fruit growing, 9, 42-43

Gallo Winery, E & J, 59
Geography, Napa Valley, 13
Geology, Napa Valley, 12-13
Geothermal activity, 10, 12, *111*
Gesford, Henry, 94, 95
Gift, George W., 74
Glass Mountain, 12, 96
Gliders, *111*
Glove industry, 82-83
Gold, 13
Gold Rush, 22, 24, 29, 43, 46, 61, 76, 84
Goodman, Carrie A., 67
Goodman, George, 67, 68
Goodman, James, 68
Goodman Library, *67,* 103
Grand Army of the Republic, San Francisco
    chapter, 73
Greystone Cellars, *55*
Greystone Winery, 9
Grgich Hills winery, 59
Grigsby, John, 28
Grigsby, T.L., 50; wine cellar of, *50*
Grigsby family, 18

Grimm Cellar, Jacob, 51; wine press of, *51*
Guisto, Louis, *95*

Hamilton, John, 30
Haraszthy, Agoston, 46-48
Hargrave, William, 28
Hatfield, Don, 6; *In the Mustard,* 6
Heitz, Joseph, 59
Hide trade, 22, *23,* 39
Higuera, Nicolas, 20, 30
Holden, Samuel, 9, 42
Hopkins, Mark, 90
Hopper, Charles, 24
Hot Springs Township, 8, 63, 87, 88, 89
Hot Sulpher Geyser Water, 91
Howell Mountain, 20, 71
Huddleston, Dave, 109; *Ehlers Lane, 109;*
    Morning Mist, 109
Hudson, David, 28
Hudspeth, James M., 30
Huntington, Collis P., 90

Indians, 13-15, 16
Inglenook, 54
Inglenook Winery, 49, 58, 59, 106, *110*
Inman Cycle Shop, Carrol, *41*
Interurban, 41

Jackson, John, *95*
Jameson Canyon Water Treatment Plant, 83
Jensen, Peter, 9, *76,* 77
Juarez, Cayetano, 8, 9, 18, *19,* 20, 28, 30, 73
Juarez Napa Band, 92
Judicial system, Napa County, 62-63, 65

Keig Shoe Factory, 83
Kellogg, Florentine E., 23, 30, 69
Kelsey, Nancy, 24
Kelseyville, 69
Kelsy, Benjamin, 28
Kelsy, Samuel, 28
Kilburn, Ralph, 21, 22, 30, 62
King, James, 63
Kittleman, Thomas, 21
Knickerbocker Number Five Company, 86
Knight's Valley, 37, 79
Knox Township, 63
Knoxville Mine, 80
Kornell, Hans, 59
Krug, Caroline Bale, 8
Krug, Charles, 8, 9, 46-49, 50, 51-52; cellar and
    vineyards of, 22, *47,* 58

Labor unrest, 82, 83
Lake Berryessa, 20
Lake County, 14, 33, 34, 37, 77
Land, Bruce, 9, 94
Land Law Act of 1851, 29
Larkyns, Harry, 75
Latour, Georges de, 52
Lawley, John, 8, 33, 34; toll house of, *33,* 77;
    toll road of, 8, 9, 32, 37, 80
Leather tanning industry, 80-82
Leese, Jacob, 20
Leffingwell, Jack, *95*
Libraries, 67-69, 104
Lick, James, 90
Literature, 77
Lodi School, *64*
Loudspeaker, invention of, 76
Lyman, W.W., Sr., 104
Lyttle, David, 97

McCrea, Fred, 59
McGowan, Edward, 63, 65
McKinney, N., 30
McLaughlin, C.E., 94
Magnavox Company, 77

Manasee family, 82
Mare Island, 94
Mare Island Naval Shipyard, 97
Mare Island Training Camp Band, 94
Marin County, 90
Markham winery, 59
Marshall, James, 8, 29
Martinez, 58, 59, 67
Martini, Louis, 59
Medical facilities, 71-73
Menefee, C.A., 11, 34
Mercury ore, 8, 80
Merritt, Ezekial, 8, 28
Methodist Church, 8, 66, 69
Methodists, 70, 71
Mexican California, 14, 16, 17, 20, 23, 24, 25,
    27-28
Mexican War, 28, 29, 61
Mexico, 16, 17, 23, 28, 29, 62
Millikan Creek, 99
Millikan Dam, 9, 83, 99
Mining, 79-80
Mission grapes, 46, 52
Mission San Francisco de Solano, *15*
Mission San Rafael, 18
Moffitt, Charles, 52
Mondavi, Robert, 58
Monterey, 61
Mont La Salle, 67; Novitiate of, *66-67*
Mont La Salle Vineyards, 67
Mt. Diablo, 90
Mount Lincoln, 89
Mount St. Helena, *12,* 13, 33, 34, 76, 77, 79,
    80
Mt. Tamalpais, 90
Musante, Giuseppe, 9, 91
Museums, 103-104
Muybridge, Eadweard, 9, 74, *75,* 76, 88
Muybridge, Flora Stone, 75

Napa, 8, 9, 30-32, 34, 37, 39, 40, 41, 42, 46,
    54, 55, 65, 66, 67, 68, 69, 71, 73, 83, 85, 90,
    92, 94, 95, 97, 98, 99; population figures,
    32-33
Napa and Vallejo Water Systems, 42
Napa Band, 94
Napa Business College, 66
Napa City-County Library, 7, 69
Napa City Directory, 83
Napa City Firehouse, 86
Napa City Gas Light Company, 9, 41, 68
Napa City Tannery, 82
Napa City Water Company, 9, 42, 99
Napa Collegiate Institute, 8, 66, 68
Napa County Directory, 74
Napa County Free Library, 68
Napa County Historical Society, 7, 67, 68, 103;
    building of, *67*
Napa County *Reporter,* 8, 74; advertisement for,
    74; office of, *74*
Napa Daily Journal, 95
Napa Fruit Company, 54; drying yards of, *54*
Napa Glove Factory, 9, 82, 85
Napa High School, 66
Napa Hotel, 65
Napa Junior College, 67
Napa Ladies' Seminary, 66
NAPA Leather, 81, 82
Napa Library Association, 9, 67
Napa Lions Club, *96*
Napa Patent Leather, 82
Napa *Register,* 8, 31, 39, 74, 94
Napa River, 8, 13, 20, 22, 30, 31, 34, 37, *38,*
    39, 42, 55, 97, 98, 101; flooding of, 98,
    99-102
Napa Sentinel, 9
Napa Soda Springs Resort, *90,* 91
Napa State Asylum for the Insane, 9, *72,* 73.

See also Napa State Hospital
Napa State Hospital, 9, 72, 73
Napa Sun, 74
Napatan Waterproof Leather, 82
Napa Township, 8, 63
Napa Valley Cooperative Winery, 59
Napa Valley Railroad, 8, 9, 39, 68; train of, *38*
Napa Valley Springs Mineral Water Company,
    91
Napa Valley Times, 9
Napa *Weekly Herald,* 74
Nash, William Huston, 42-43, 65
National Industrial Recovery Act, 96
Native Sons of the Golden West, 104
Newspapers, 74. *See also* individual names of
    newspapers
New York Meat Market, *42*
Nichellini Winery, 44
Niebaum, Gustave, 49, 50, 54, 59, 110

Oakland, 82
Oak Mound School, 66
Oat Hill mine, 80, 85
Oats, 13
Old Faithful geyser, *111*
Olive production, 43, 54
Oregon City, 69
Oroville, 95
Osborne, Fanny, 77

Pacheteau's Original Hot Springs, 90
Pachett, J.M., 46, 48
Pacific Echo, 74
Pacific Union College, 20, 67, 96
Palisades mine, 9, 80
Palmer, L.L., 46
Parker, H.C., 39; residence and ranch of, *38*
Parrott, Tiburcio, 54
Patwin Indians, 13, 16
Paul Pry (steamship), 39
Pecota Winery, Robert, 59
Perrier, 91
Petaluma, 39
Petrified Forest, *91*
Phoenix Mining Company, 8, 80
Phylloxera, 9, 43, 51, 52, 54
Pierce, Harrison, 8, 28, 30
Pioneer Engine Company, 62
Pithie, R.H., 34
Pomo Indians, 11, 16
Poncietta, Walter, *95*
Pope, Julian, 20
Pope Street Bridge, 34
Pope Valley, 20
Population figures: Napa County, 33; Napa
    Valley, 42
Pratt, W.A., 71
Presbyterians, 70
Pridham, Edwin, 9, *76,* 77
Prohibition, 9, 58, 59, 95; repeal of, 96
Prouty, Harry, 94
Prouty, Raymond, 94
Prune production, 13, 43, 54
Public Works Administration, 96
Putah Creek, 34
Putah Creek Bridge, 34, *35*

Queen of the Valley Hospital, 73
Quicksilver, 39, 80

Rancho Carne Humana, 8, 21
Rancho Catacula, 8, 24
Rancho Caymus, 8, 17, 18, 20, 30
Rancho de la Jota, 20
Rancho Entre Napa, 20
Rancho Huichica, 20
Rancho period, 17, 20, 23, 24, 46
Rancho Tulucay, 8, 18, 20

Raymond, E.H., 83
Raymond, R., 83
Red Cross, 95
Red Hill mine, 80
Religion, 69-71. *See also* individual names of churches
Resorts, 88-91. *See also* individual names of resorts
Richie Block, *110*
Riley, Bennett, 30, 61
Robert Louis Stevenson Memorial State Park, 7, 77
Robert Louis Stevenson Museum, 104
Roberts, Leonard, *95*
Robinson, E. John, 2; *Harvest Gold, 2-3*
Rodriguez, Damaso, 20
Roosevelt, Franklin D., 95, 96
Rough Rider Clothing Manufacturers, 83
Rural Health Retreat, 71
Russell, Charles, 22
Russian American Company, 14
Russian Orthodox, 70; church of, 71
Russian settlement, 17, 46, 71
Rutherford, 8, 17, *32,* 49, 52, 59, 85, 106
Rutherford, Elizabeth, 32
Rutherford, Thomas, 32
Rutherford Vintners, 59

Sacramento, 8, 27, 28, 39, 63, 94
Sacramento (ship), 8, 37
Sacramento Valley, 13
St. Helena, 8, 12, 20, *32,* 33, 34, *40,* 41, 48, 54, 56, 64, 66, 69, 71, *78,* 83, 85, 103, 104, 110
St. Helena (ship), 12
St. Helena baseball team, *82*
St. Helena Catholic Church, *69*
St. Helena Club, 49
St. Helena Grape Growers Coop winery, 59
St. Helena Hospital and Health Center, 20, 71
St. Helena Library, 9, *68,* 104
St. Helena Methodist Church, 70
St. Helena Photogram, 94
St. Helena Sanitarium, 9, *71*
St. Helena Star, 9, 48, 74, 75; office of, *75*
St. Helena Township, 63

St. Helena Viticultural Club, 9, 52
St. Helena Wine Library, 68, 104
Sanchez, José, 8, 16
San Diego, 45
San Francisco, 37, 39, 40, 52, 56, 57, 58, 63, 65, 69, 75, 77, 83, 85, 86, 87, 88, 89
San Francisco, Napa and Calistoga Railroad Company, 40
San Francisco Bay, 13
San Francisco de Solano Mission, 13, 16, 18, 69, 71
San Jose, 66
San Mateo, 46
San Pablo Bay, 13
Santa Clara County, 29
Santa Rosa, 57, 83
'Sante Water Company, A., 91
Sawyer, B.F., 80
Sawyer, F.A., 80
Sawyer Tanning Company, 9, 80, 82; employees of, *81;* tannery of, *81,* 82
Schram, Jacob, 50, 54, 77
Schramsburg, 54, 85
Sebastopol, 30. *See also* Yountville
Sellars, J.A., 63
Serra, Juniperro, 45
Seventh Day Adventist Church, 9, 71
Seventh-day Adventists, 67, 71
Sharpsteen, Ben, 103, 104
Sharpsteen Museum, 90, 104
Shoe industry, 83
Shurtleff, Benjamin, 71, 73
Shurtleff Hospital, 9, 71, 73
Silver, 13, 80
Silverado City, 80
Silverado Hotel, 80
Silverado mine, 77, 79
Silverado Trail, 34, 96
Silver Rush, 79
Simonds, Samuel, 69
Smallpox epidemic, 8, 16
Smith, Jedediah, 25
Smith, Joseph, 87
Soberanes, Maria Ignacia, 20
Solano County, 14

Sonoma, 8, 15, 16, 17, 18, 20, 26, 28, 47, 48
Sonoma County, 14, 37
Sonoma State Historic Park, 15
Sonoma Valley, 20, 46, 51
Soscol, 39, 79, 90
Soscol Wharf, 90
Southern Pacific Railroad, 39, 82; depot of, 94, 95
South Primary School, *60*
Spain, 17
Spanish California, 15-16
Spear, Nathan, 23
Spiers, William, 34, 37
Stanford, Leland, 75, 90
Stanislaus River, 87
Starke, John E., 30
Stevenson, Robert Louis, 9, *76,* 77, 79, 80; *Silverado Squatters,* 9, 76, 77, 80; *Treasure Island,* 9, 77
Still, Henry, 32, 33
Stockton, 8, 66, 73
Stone, Flora, 75
Storm, Peter, *26*
Strauss clothing store, Abe, *42*
Sutter's Fort, 27, 28, 29
Sutterville, 88. *See also* Sacramento

Tallow trade, 22, *23*
Taylor, Duckworth and Company, 83
Third Street Bridge, *97*
Thompson, Joseph P., 31
Thompson, T.H., 73
Tourism, 59, 90-91, 103, 112
Transportation, 34-40, 90
Trubody, John, 31
Tubbs, A.L., 95
Tucker, Reason P., 28, *29*
Tucker family, 104
Tulocay Cemetery, 9, *18,* 20
Tychson, Josephine, 104

U.S.S. *Crownblock,* 97
U.S.S. *Whipstock,* 97
Uncle Sam Cellar, 55
United Vintners, 59

University of the Pacific, 8, 66
Utility service, 41-42

Vailima Foundation, 104
Vallejo, 40, 75, 97, 99
Vallejo, Benecia, and Napa Valley Railroad Company, 40, 41
Vallejo, Mariano, 16, 17, 18, 20, 24, 28, 30, 31, 46, *88*
Vallejo, Salvador, 20, 28
Victory Hospital, 73
Victory Memorial Hospital, 73
Villa Parrott, *54*
Viticultural Commissioners, State Board of, 52

Walker, Joseph, 24, 25
Wappo Indians, 8, 13, 14, 16
Water supply, 98-99, 103
Weinberger's Cellar, John C., 52, *53*
Wheat, growing of, 13, 23-24, 29, 42, 43
Whilton, Jesse, 30
White, Asa, 69
White Church, *69*
White Sulpher Springs Resort, 88, 91
Wilson, Woodrow, 58, 95
Wine, shipping of, 39
Wine industry, 13, 44-59, 110
Wine press, *44*
Wineries. See individual wineries
Wine tasting, 59
Wine Train, 9, 40
Works Progress Administration, 97
World War I, 9, 80, 93-95, 96
World War II, 58, 91, 96, 97-98, 99

Yellow Jacket mine, 75
Yerba Buena, 23
Young, Brigham, 88
Yount, George Calvert, 8, *17,* 18, 20, 24, 30, 32
Yount Jorge Concepcion, 18. *See also* Yount, George Calvert
Yount Grist Mill, 24
Yount Township, 8, 63
Yountville, 9, 17, 18, 30, 54, 73